Praise for PIVOT.

"*PIVOT.* is a must read for anyone who struggles with finding their passion during uncertain times. Call it a book. Call it a devotional. Whatever you call it, it is the 21st century playbook on triumph, success, and self-belief—against the odds. You will laugh, cry, and wave your hands in the air. Quiet the voice of fear and self-doubt and turn the page."

Karen Arrington
NAACP Image Award-Winning Author, Mentor,
Philanthropist, Founder of Miss Black USA Pageant

"The COVID epidemic left few untouched, many forever changed and each of us with stories to tell. This book curates personal COVID stories of joy, loss, love, laughter, and lessons learned. Each tale rings of familiarity and hopefulness—offering a soothing balm to ease the way forward."

Ambassador Ertharin Cousin
Food Systems for the Future
President and Co-Founder

"The pivotal moments shared in this book remind me of the courage and determination required to succeed in life. Own your journey and design your life's plan with *PIVOT.* as a guiding light."

Deb Elam
President & CEO, Corporate Playbook
Global Chief Diversity Officer, GE (retired)

"The stories that these writers share show us how we can discover new meaning for our lives, even in the darkest days."

Anita F. Hill
University Professor, Legal Scholar and Advocate

"Navigating the pandemic did not put on pause navigating life! I am confident that you will find yourself, as I did, relating to moments in these stories that required us to PIVOT. Commendations to the authors who were transparent yet extremely encouraging to people who will find new or renewed passion and purpose through this book."

Karla Munden
Chief Audit Executive
Lincoln Financial Group

"*PIVOT.* is on point!!! As someone whose life's work has been focused on preserving African American life, history and culture through the recording of the stories of African American leaders both well known and unsung, the stories found in *PIVOT.* reflect the brilliance of its authors. For its readers, *PIVOT.* will be transformational!"

Julieanna Richardson
Founder & President, The HistoryMakers

PIVOT.

How the pandemic pushed **Women** to their passion

Collection of Stories Compiled by
Sharon P. Jarrett and
Jylla Moore Tearte, Ph.D.

CRYSTAL STAIRS
PUBLISHERS

PIVOT.
How the pandemic pushed Women to their passion

Compilers and Contributing Authors: Sharon P. Jarrett and Jylla Moore Tearte, Ph.D. **Contributing Authors:** Marjorie A. Kinard, Chonya Johnson, Alana Ward Robinson, Dr. Stacie NC Grant, Helen Hope Kimbrough, Gigi Gilliard, Marilyn Johnson, Rev. Teraleen Campbell, Marie Turner McCleave, Tamara McGill McFarland, Natasha Sunday Clarke, Audrey Washington, Monique N. Tookes, Melissa I. Walton Jones, Kristin Harper, Dr. Jeri Dyson, Anjylla Y. Foster, Ph.D., Vesta Godwin Clark.

Cover art by Dreama Fine Art.
Cover design and interior page layout by the Ink Studio

ISBN 978-1-940131-31-3 (paperback)
ISBN 978-1-940131-32-0 (ebook)

Library of Congress Control Number: 2021918083

Crystal Stairs Publishers, Crystal Stairs, Inc.
P. O. Box 690820; Charlotte, NC 28227
Publishers@Crystal-Stairs.com

CRYSTAL STAIRS PUBLISHERS

For special orders, quantity sales, corporate sales, trade or wholesale sales, please contact the publisher at CustomerService@Crystal-Stairs.com

Printed in the United States of America

PIVOT. *is dedicated to everyone who has a story to release into the universe as a means to help others find a path of light to their passion and purpose.*

"You have to know how to pivot, you have to step back, get on the balcony, survey the scene, throw out what you know or what you think you know and then find the answer that's going to fit this issue right here."

– Bishop Vashti Murphy McKenzie

Contents

Introduction

Early one morning, Sharon Jarrett posted a very transparent social media post that captured my attention. I immediately sent her a text message, "Your post is a book. Are you interested in working with me to publish a book?" Her immediate response was, "Let's do it! When can we talk?" At 4:30 P.M., July 15, 2021, we talked on the phone and wondered if other women had similar stories. In that pivotal moment, the genesis of this book was born.

Invitations to participate were extended to women who we knew were storytellers, but we had no clue if they had a potential story that fit the theme and mission. The conversations that followed were met with excitement and "Oh yes! I have a story!" The responses were immediate and conversations that ensued were as gut-wrenching as Sharon's initial post. Testimonies were shared that were as unexpected as the pandemic itself, if not more so. The revelation of a potential book evolved into what we believe is an assignment that we worked to fulfill with maniacal focus and a deep commitment to helping others with authentic stories like the women featured in these pages. It is in discovering the power of story and the sharing of conversations, that we found purpose in encouraging others to PIVOT.

As we explored the title and defined the work we would curate, we settled on a word that spoke in a resounding manner— PIVOT. Initially, we worked with PIVOT. (the period is intentional) as though it were a noun, a simple word. As we dug deep into the stories, however, we felt a shift—PIVOT is an action verb. Each author's story in this work illuminates that distinction.

In this book are the authentic voices of the authors with unfiltered stories that were sequestered in their hearts and souls. Their personal experiences are the backdrop and frame of reference for the moments of pause and insight they pour out. The authors share with a myriad of situations relative to family, health, grief, fear, caregiving, mental health, business model shifts, entrepreneurship, toxic environments, patience, and virtual learning.

We asked for stories that would seek to inspire others and that would open eyes to find the light beyond the darkest curtains. Collectively, the stories are a woven tapestry of narratives that evoke a-ha moments for readers, embraces them in the truth that they are not alone, and challenges them to dive into and walk boldly into their own pivotal moment. The request to the authors was to reach deep to help someone find themselves in the story so that they might "PIVOT" out of the pandemic tunnel. They succeeded in doing that and in making a clarion call to harness belief, faith, focus, grit, perseverance, and determination to overcome.

The words of Paul Laurence Dunbar's original circa 1895 poem, *We Wear the Mask*, were later interpreted in spoken word by Dr. Maya Angelou. They captured the deep emotions and experiences that lie beneath masks that people wear. These emotions are not often communicated in words but via the language of piercing eyes that appear above the mask of being tired, weary, peaceful, wondering, and possibly trusting. The cover art by Artist Dreama Kemp calls us to remember that we wear masks! Women have worn varied proverbial masks for centuries and physical masks continue to cover the burden of hidden emotions. This collection of stories penetrated the masks of 20 women so that other masked emotions might be removed with one critical pivot.

For some of the authors, this book is the first time their story has been told. For others, preaching and teaching were condensed into revelations of personal self-care and created effectual pauses in busy and over-scheduled lives. For some was the discovery or the push into their passion and purpose. The collective cry throughout is that tough times don't last always; you can PIVOT.

Lest we forget the months of shutdown and the fear of the spread of the initial strain of the virus, we will repeat so many of the threats that precipitated the shutdown of our economy. If we allow our one pandemic moment in time to escape our consciousness, we will not appreciate from whence we have come and sink back into the fear and uncertainty of the path forward. If we determine that we will strengthen how we communicate beneath the mask, we will spread narratives that will push people to their passion. We must still rise up to claim our purpose by never ceasing to fight for our dreams.

The journey is not over. There are stories yet to be told. Untold stories that may never find the light. We who wear the mask must be ever ready to help somebody as we journey through life. We are still the keeper of our brothers and sisters. We must tackle the social ills and be diligent in social advocacy for issues that raise their notorious heads. This book reminds you that despite this pandemic or any challenge before you, you can still write a different ending to your story. The words herein are designed to support and lift you as you climb out of the trenches of the pandemic. This book invites you to adopt and adapt pages from the authors' stories to recall, reflect, renew and react with a plan of action to PIVOT.

There is power in the story. We ask that you spark conversations with *PIVOT.* Call up circles of friends or a forgotten acquaintance or relative and decide that you will write a story together of "how you got over". Of how you got to the other side to find your passion. Adopt a cause where you can be the light via a donation of time, talent, and/or treasure. Let's ignite the movement toward service above self while using self as an anchor to lift as we climb. Let's make sure *PIVOT.* finds a HOME in your actions.

– Jylla Moore Tearte, Ph.D.

In The Beginning

I'm Not Okay!! And That's Okay Too!

By Sharon P. Jarrett

I am known for my no-nonsense yet upbeat personality (on most days) and my ability to communicate my expectations of others (every day). While excellence and professionalism have always been the cornerstones of my career, I'm also that "let's keep it 100% real" family member, girlfriend, and co-worker whom you never have to guess what's on her mind. My eyes can give you complete instructions on how to interact with me without my mouth saying one word. Can I get a witness? My Uncle Ezell often refers to me as his sister's mean daughter (LOL). Whatever, man! However, not unlike others, this pandemic broke my spirit!

Back in March of 2020, 72 hours prior to my departure to Paris, France to produce a series of events over a seven-day period, my team had to cancel our flights. We believed this virus thing would be over within a few weeks, and we would resume our travel plans. You know the rest of the story; for the next 16 months, we were all grounded! NO TRAVEL. NO PEOPLE. NO LIVE EVENTS. My usual work from home A-L-O-N-E routine, which had been in existence for 10 years, was abruptly revised with my entire family of GROWN and WANNA BE GROWN folks working and living together 24 hours a day, seven days a week. It was fun initially, but that didn't last long. As the pandemic grew, my patience, no BS-meter and lack of a desire to interact with humans became a challenge. The sofa was a far more enjoyable choice.

Admittedly, I wasn't the nicest person in our house and often stayed secluded in my office. Logging on to social media was like reading daily obituary pages, so I chose to limit my time there. This went on for several months. I did enough to satisfy existing clients, but my creativity was at an all-time low and I walked away from exciting business opportunities because quite frankly, I just didn't feel up to it. I am forever grateful that my immediate family could sense that something wasn't right and gave me the space to just BE. My kids (excuse me, young adults) learned when not to enter my office to ask me for anything - *enter Mommy Guilt.* My parents, sister, Godparents, and closest friends called more than usual, and when I did feel like picking up the phone (which wasn't often), they never pressed me about my "I'm okay" response to their never-ending question, "What's wrong?"

Just by deciding to prioritize my own self-care (body, mind, and soul), I went from not knowing what to do or pray for, to daily, sometimes hourly conversations with God about what He/She wanted for me next.

This went on for months and then I hit my personal pandemic wall. I felt like if one, just O.N.E more person on a virtual call said, "You're muted _____. Please turn your mic on," I would throw my laptop through the window. Seriously, I identified a nice spot in the grass outside of my office window that would be a great place for it to land. Can you relate? Well on the day that it almost happened, I knew I had to do something. I had produced enough conferences with topics on "LIVING YOUR BEST

LIFE" to know that if I didn't RELAX, RELATE and RELEASE soon, there was going to be some furniture moving around in my house! I was living on the verge of, "I wish a _____would!"

For several weeks, feeling tired and totally overwhelmed, I removed myself from almost everything, and I spent time with myself, my Bible, and a culturally competent therapist. During this time my self-care became a non-negotiable priority. My husband deserves an award for the extra dose of patience that was required during this season and when that wasn't enough, he provided laughter. The night he missed a step and slid down the staircase holding a full plate of pasta, which was still intact when he reached the bottom step, was GOLD for the television show *America's Funniest Home Videos*! I don't think we had laughed that hard together in years, it was so good for my soul!

I will never forget some of my business besties, who always supported my endeavors, and usually saw me at my best, individually reached out to me to simply check-in because they too could sense something wasn't right. A few offered expertise in their chosen fields by inviting me to private brainstorming sessions, VIP days, and clarity sessions that I desperately needed. I definitely plan to redeem them all and appreciate their willingness to seek me out and check up on me when I just wanted to be left alone. Their genuine kindness and concern WITHOUT JUDGMENT meant more to me than they will ever know.

For my friends who follow my personal social media pages closely, I'm sure they noticed during this season, that I wasn't posting as much; while I was working through my stuff, my circle was holding a space for me, and God was engineering things on my behalf. Just by deciding to prioritize my own self-care (body, mind, and soul), I went from not knowing what to do or pray for, to daily, sometimes hourly conversations with God about what He/She wanted for me next. This has been a mind-blowing experience that has allowed me to re-emerge more aware than ever about what's possible. Some might say that the pandemic pushed me to my true event passion. I have received countless good wishes on my recent accomplishments, such as my election to the Global Board of Trustees for Meeting Professionals International (MPI) which is the largest meeting and event industry association worldwide, in addition to adding new and exciting clients to my roster. GOD IS SO GOOD! All of the good wishes warmed my heart and were another signal for me that my mini, unannounced sabbatical, was necessary and time well spent. I am excited, and clear on my assignment and my creativity is back in overdrive. I can't wait to share all the juicy stuff God and I have planned. Until then, I implore you to make self-care a non-negotiable priority and stop saying you're okay when you are not! I hope this helps somebody. Did any of this resonate with you? We cannot keep pretending that we are okay! Your mental wellness is critical, do not let self-care be the missing piece to your happiness.

I can't wait to share all the juicy stuff God and I have planned. Until then, I implore you to make self-care a non-negotiable priority and stop saying you're okay when you are not!

Lest We Forget

Faith, Peace and Trust During Tumultuous Times

By Marjorie A. Kinard

I was a 77-year-old woman, living a life of stability, involved in my church, engaged in organizational leadership, and enjoying the love of family from a quiet neighborhood in Maryland. There I was a well-traveled, educated, and respected person in my community when COVID-19 shook most of us up. I knew something was brewing in the atmosphere because of what I read in the newspapers, saw on television, and observed on social media. The news talked about the pandemic's effects around the world. For some reason, those in the United States did not take the first warnings seriously based on how COVID-19 was ravaging other countries. I do not know if we thought we were immune to it, or if we thought it would not devastate us in the same way.

I remembered hearing about the correlation of the coronavirus invasion to the influenza pandemic of 1918. Through articles and videos about it, I learned what it had done to communities across our country. Of course, in those days, the scientific knowledge about the spread of diseases, where they originate, and what we need to do to be safe, was not as sound as it is today. One thing

I do know, history repeats itself, and if you are not prepared, and if you do not learn from history, you are the loser.

The Centers for Disease Control and Prevention worked extremely hard, (in my opinion), to keep us informed, giving best practices for keeping ourselves healthy, and providing continuous new findings through daily reports about the virus. President Donald Trump, for some reason, did not want us to know the full extent of the danger of this pandemic, and was slow in taking the disease seriously. I think that if he had acted earlier in responding to the suggestions of the experts, perhaps more lives could have been saved. He rejected the use of masks, and when vaccines were developed, he played down the importance of getting the shots. He created division in the land which caused ambivalence about the seriousness of what we were facing. While he was in denial, we were seeing horrific broadcasts announcing tens of thousands of deaths. Many of the early deaths were the elderly. We saw people dying in hospitals, without the support of their families. There were so many deaths that hospitals and morgues could not contain them. Many bodies were put in body bags and stored in refrigerated trucks. Families could not, in some cases, claim their loved ones, nor could funerals be held. Funeral homes could not accommodate the large numbers of services required and families were in a quandary, not knowing what to do.

> The Pandemic of 2020 changed the trajectory in the lives of everyone I know. We were afraid. We were stunned. We did not know which way to turn.

The Pandemic of 2020 changed the trajectory in the lives of everyone I know. We were afraid. We were stunned. We did not know which way to turn. Those in my age group were quick to obey the guidelines for safety. As time went on, those who were hesitant realized that these were serious times and that being resistant to those guidelines meant death to members of their families. Initially, there was no test to determine who had the disease, so we quarantined ourselves and used germ killers as health measures. We sprayed ourselves with alcohol, and other germ repellants, we increased our supplies of food, toilet paper, paper towels, water. We stayed in the house and tried not to go outside if at all possible. We wore masks around those who lived outside of our homes.

The most difficult part of the quarantine for me was that I could not see my family. I am a widow, with three adult daughters, a son-in-law, and five grandchildren. Not being able to see or touch them was exceedingly difficult. On my 78th birthday, my daughter who lives in Hampton, Virginia, drove to my home, in Maryland, with three of my grandchildren to see me. They could not come into the house, so I sat on the front porch and we all stayed outside, without touching and talked from a distance. That was so very hard.

> The most difficult part of the quarantine for me was that I could not see my family. I am a widow, with three adult daughters, a son-in-law, and five grandchildren. Not being able to see or touch them was exceedingly difficult.

As time went on, it became increasingly more difficult not to do the things I was used to doing. I missed going to church to worship in a brick-and-mortar building, seeing my friends there, laughing, talking, and getting caught up on what was going on in their lives. I missed taking Communion, the bread and wine, which we experienced each first Sunday of the month. I missed going to my sorority meetings and other organizational meetings. I thank God for Zoom, along with other apps which allowed us to interact with one another. Our lives became videoconference centered for church services, meetings of every type, birthday parties, conferences, workshops, and other important events. Social media became very important to our existence during this time. Many people worked from home, during that time, and others lost their jobs.

It is amazing how quickly one gets used to a new routine. It is amazing how quickly we can get used to a new way of doing things and we begin to forget those things we thought were so important to us.

The public school systems closed to face-to-face classes for children in elementary, junior high, and high schools. I traveled to Hampton, Virginia, to be with my granddaughters to make certain that someone was with them through the online schooling process in the early phase of their learning. What a rich experience. Had it not been for the pandemic, there would have been no reason for me to spend three months with them to encourage and be a resource to them while their parents worked. I also traveled to North Carolina, with my daughter, to take my third grandson to college. It was his freshman year, and I wanted to make certain that he arrived safely, and I wanted to see his dorm and assure him he had what he needed to be successful. Even though he lived on campus, most of his classes were online at North Carolina A & T State University. My second grandson went to Livingstone College for his junior year, alone.

I lost family members and friends during the pandemic. We all became closer to God and prayed for one another. My oldest grandson and granddaughter tested positive for COVID-19 and were quarantined for two weeks. I was beside myself with worry about them. As a matter of fact, I worried about all of my children and grandchildren. I worried about my two sisters and my nieces and nephews. I prayed for my friends near and far. When my brother was near death from liver cancer, I traveled to Fort Wayne, Indiana, to see him. I knew about the quarantine and the difficulty of seeing loved ones in the hospital, but that was my brother. My daughter, and I (with the help of my niece/his daughter who is a Ph.D. Nurse), were able to see him during his last hours. We had a memorial for him via Zoom. There were family members in attendance from all around the country.

I was hesitant about taking the COVID-19 vaccine. I pondered it for months, before deciding I had to take it. I needed to be an example for my family and friends who had not made the decision. Many were waiting to see what I was going to do. I am so thankful that I did, because a month following my last vaccine, I found myself in the hospital, twice. The second visit was for a total hip replacement. Had I not taken the vaccine, my treatment protocols, I understand, would have been much different.

As an elder, I am eternally grateful for life, strength, and the promise of a better tomorrow.

I turned 79 years old in June 2021. We are still in the midst of the pandemic. I am thankful to God that I have made it to this point. I am still very careful about wearing my mask, taking my vitamins to build my immune system, going out in crowds and around people I do not know. I continue to check on my family and friends and share notes about how we can safely sustain our lives during this critical time. As an elder, I am eternally grateful for life, strength, and the promise of a better tomorrow. We are not out of the woods yet, because another strain of the virus swept over the nation. But this one thing I know, God is the ultimate power. God has control, therefore I have peace and trust in Him.

Arrested with Purpose

By Chonya Johnson

Why am I here? What am I supposed to really do on this Earth? I asked these questions repeatedly during my advocacy days on Capitol Hill and even recently during lobby days for Bread for the World, a non-profit organization battling food insecurity. I listened intently and studied others for clues about my next right action, aligned with my purpose.

One of America's monumental occasions, particularly for black women, occurred on January 20, 2021. The date is indelibly etched in my memory. I watched the long-awaited Inauguration Day for Vice President Kamala Harris, from a hospital bed. I had contracted the life-changing virus – COVID-19. I was arrested by the virus and sentenced to six days in intensive care. I was fighting for my life; yet did not tell many people. In fact, most will only know of my battle with the coronavirus, upon reading these words.

I was sitting in a hospital bed with tubes and oxygen flowing through them – to keep me alive. I was fighting for my life while witnessing the first black woman be sworn in as Vice President of the United States. I was supposed to be there; cheering, clapping, and hugging my fellow sisters. We canvassed together the year prior to the election in the battleground states. I had also worked phone banks and donated financially to the campaign to elect her and then presidential candidate Joe Biden. Despite the pushback from some in the black community, I stressed the importance of the 2020 Presidential Election. I believed her election into one of the highest offices in the United States was necessary for black women and girls, a pivotal group that has been fighting for years to be seen. At that moment, as she took the oath of office, we would be front and center for the world to see our greatness; and being authentically ourselves from a wide range of backgrounds. We would be seen.

I remember vividly making my way to the bathroom one day, and as I looked in the mirror, I saw terror in my eyes. My life flashed before me.

Barely breathing, slumped over the side of my bed, I thought about how I received my positive COVID-19 diagnosis. My heart sank, I cried into my pillow and summoned my daughter to drive me to the hospital. It was real. I had contracted COVID-19. As much as I wanted to hang in there – I could no longer bear trying to gasp for air or walk (more like crawl) to the bathroom to avoid embarrassing accidents. My body had never failed me in this way. I'd never had pneumonia or any illness that took me down like COVID. I was terrified.

I remember vividly making my way to the bathroom one day, and as I looked in the mirror, I saw terror in my eyes. My life flashed before me. I remember crying out to God, "You aren't finished with me yet God! Why me?" After months on lockdown and being vigilant about being careful! Why? Why me? I told God, and myself, "I do not want to die like this; and I do not want to die now."

Standing in the bathroom, afraid, not wanting to go to the hospital for fear of dying at 47 years old, I knew I had to do something. I had seen many news stories of people dying and it was not just older people. COVID was not discriminating. I reluctantly made the wiser choice and called out to Cass (my daughter) who didn't even have a learner's permit and asked her to drive me to the Howard County emergency room.

I couldn't even walk to the doors. I was panting and crying. I was scared as hell, thinking my life would end in that emergency room. I would go to God in leopard pajamas with ashy feet because I was too exhausted to use lotion in days past. Cass was a strong trooper. She entered the double doors and asked the security officer for a wheelchair to help her mom. Within seconds, she wheeled me in before hospital staff asked her to leave quickly. She kissed me on the top of my head and said, "bye Mom; love you!" Hospital staff rolled me to an intake window to check in. I couldn't get any words out because I couldn't breathe and was fatigued from sleepless nights of coughing uncontrollably.

I handed the receptionist my identification and insurance cards and begged, "please get me to a doctor." It seemed in a moment, a doctor came over, held my hand, and offered encouragement. She said, "You are going to get through this." She must have noticed the despair and anxiety on my face. I said softly, "I don't want to die yet."

I was admitted quickly with a bed assignment in the ER. They ran a full body scan, x-rays, and more; before administering oxygen, which helped me immensely. The next day I was given a private room and the results of my tests, the prognosis was it would be at least six days before they could release me because my lungs, heart rate, and blood pressure were not operating properly. I was poked with so many needles and given a sleep aid because my anxiety was causing me to fear the worst constantly. I still cannot recall all the details of the ordeal, and, in some ways, I don't want to relive the pain of knowing that my purpose was almost aborted.

But God said, "Not yet!"

Days later - I was still alive, and I had a chance to go deep into the recesses of my mind and soul. I had to draw from years of Sunday School at Greater St. Stephens where I learned about faith and recall all the times God had shown up for me despite my trying to do it Chonya's way. I thought long and hard about Cassie and whether she would be okay if I had died, would the resources that I'd left be enough; so many questions bombarded me. I then looked deeper inside and said to myself I had to have a little more faith. I spoke what I believed to be true, God was not done with me yet. Those words were my daily declaration and affirmation on my death and wellness bed. I shall live and not die was on my heart.

> After six days in the ICU, I became more overwhelmed and arrested with purpose. I thanked God for another chance to live on purpose.

After six days in the ICU, I became more overwhelmed and arrested with purpose. I thanked God for another chance to live on purpose. I committed wholeheartedly to care for myself better. I walk three miles three to five times a week. I show up and speak up in spaces where food insecurity is at higher rates for minorities because of the color of their skin. I also committed to enjoying a radical "Do What Sets Your Soul on Fire" soul care journey (during the pandemic), which included three visits to the beaches of St. Croix and a rendezvous in Paris.

I am arrested with purpose daily and realize I only have one life to live, and I will live on purpose for a purpose. Being my best self is the gift I can give. I encourage you to speak up and stand up in sharing your authenticity with the world.

A Fearful Night of Terror

By Alana Ward Robinson

My husband and I spent over 90 days of the COVID-19 lock-down in our condo in downtown Chicago. Just the two of us. We also owned a place on the other side of the lake in Michigan – but we decided that staying downtown was the best option for us. After all, if by chance we did become infected, we would be close to our doctors, the hospital and have easier access to care.

During this time, all of the common areas in our condo building were shut down. No gym. No pool. No lounge. Nothing. Without access to the building's condo balcony on the ninth floor, we could not go outside at all. I mean at all. 90 days inside. Phew!

Before the pandemic, the view from our 13th-floor windows always included families out walking with children, children walking to and from school, people going to and from work or walking their dogs, shoppers, and tourists.

During the lockdown – all of that changed. No people. No taxis. None of the usual downtown noise. It was a big adjustment (and did I say that we did this for 90 days?!!). We received the occasional Amazon package deliveries and literally soaked the boxes with disinfectant before opening them. Let me tell you, extended confinement in a small space with no access to fresh air was rough. 90 days. 90 days. On warmer days, we could at least open our windows to get some fresh air.

So how did we manage to get groceries? I was an Instacart phenom – but choices were limited and deliveries from them were scheduled days out. Our youngest son and his family lived in the Chicago area, so every two weeks, he and his family would shop our list and bring us groceries. On delivery day, we would mask up and go down to the lobby to look directly in his eyes and say thanks. No hugs allowed. To see my son and not be able to hug him was such a dreadful feeling. This. Was. So. Hard.

But that night, I heard continuous sirens. Even with my eyes closed – it just felt like this was over the top. The sirens kept getting louder and louder. I knew something wasn't right.

Sometimes we got to walk outside of the building to see our daughter-in-law and grandsons in the car. But we didn't dare get too close. We are both over 65 years old and considered high risk for COVID. Once we would make the elevator ride back up to our condo, I would cry. My arms ached from the bags. My heart ached, I wanted to hug my family. Facetime or Zoom was no match for being in the physical presence of family. No match at all!

And then there was our business. As independent consultants for more than 15 years, we had established solid relationships with our clients and teammates. Our team managed to conduct business in a seamless manner, kept our projects on track, and delivered our consulting services virtually. We even started new engagements without having to get on a plane or spend nights in hotels.

For entertainment, we watched movie after movie – several on repeat. *Coming to America, Coming to America II*, and *Black Panther* were favorites. Cute romance movies became a thing. Multiple mind-blowing documentaries kept us engaged. We played games, too: dominoes, checkers, and spades. Our games would sometimes end abruptly if my husband decided to cheat! We cooked every day! So not normal for us. We tried out long-forgotten culinary skills. Well, at least for me. My specialty became eating and then critiquing his meals. I made homemade sweet potato pies which are his favorite! Fabulous – if I do say so myself!

We tried to stay positive, did what was expected, and counted on our faith for hope and patience. But the days seemed to last longer, and the nights were way too short. Weekdays were filled with one Zoom call after another. Nights and weekends for family Zoom calls became our new normal.

One Saturday night, in late May 2020, we both went to bed around 10 P.M. Hearing an ambulance or police siren every day or any time of the day comes with living downtown – I was used to it. But that night, I heard continuous sirens. Even with my eyes closed – it just felt like this was over the top. The sirens kept getting louder and louder. I knew something wasn't right. I got out of bed, looked outside my bedroom window and I saw a ton of commotion on the street below. Sleepy and confused, but still a little nosey, I went to the living room – with windows on two walls – my view was much better there.

What did I see? I saw crowds of people and lots of cars lined up in formation with their trunks open. What was going on? I flew back to the bedroom and shook my husband – telling him that he had to get up and "get up NOW!" I got my phone and started recording the chaos. Hubby called down to the front desk and the doorman told him the police had been notified and the building management had decided to lock up the building and turn off all the lights in the lobby. At this point, we turned on the news. Holy Moly! Downtown Chicago was under siege with property damage and retail looting going on everywhere.

I think I was in shock – but I was still at the windows – mesmerized by what I was seeing. A young man was walking down the street with an ax. He proceeded to beat on the window of the Intermix store across the street from our building enough times to shatter the glass. Once he got the opening big enough – several people rushed in the store, opened the doors, and left with armfuls of clothes to load up in the trunks of the waiting cars. After a few trips back and forth, the car trunks were full. By now, I have my son on the phone and I'm giving him a play-by-play of what's going on. All of a sudden – S&^T!! We heard gunshots, people scattered, and all the cars sped off. My son was yelling that I needed to move away from the windows. I couldn't. This was great TV!

But the cars came back. The breaking of store windows, looting of merchandise, and loading it into cars continued for a couple of hours. The cars would be side-by-side, at least four across and several rows long. As soon as one row was done, they left and the next row of four came to the front. It was organized. It was planned. It was terrifying. The precision of execution was mind-boggling!

There were no police in sight during this entire time. Now, we were really scared and started talking about how to protect ourselves, how to get out of the building, and all sorts of "what ifs." Now was THE time to make some decisions!

We blocked our entry door with furniture, packed a small bag, and went back to bed praying that we would be okay to leave the next morning. We decided to leave downtown and go to our home in Michigan. We put our bags in the car and exited our parking garage in what felt like a stealth move. The destruction we saw on our way out of the city was - I cannot even describe it. Awful? Devastating? Downright scary? All of that. I felt like we didn't even breathe until we were safely on Highway 94 headed to Michigan.

Well, 90 days of isolation coupled with an intense night of chaos prompted us to think about so many things. We thought about the crowds of people looting with no masks on, visibly recorded on store cameras, and clearly fearless. We couldn't help but think that what we saw was rehearsed and pre-planned. We saw that the designated roles (glass breaker, looter, driver, gun signals that prompted movement) and the sequence of actions were executed flawlessly. And we wondered. Who was the mastermind of the chaos? What motivated this behavior? We will never know. How could all of this disruption and damage occur with NO intervention by cops?

But what we do know is that being isolated is lonely. We do know that family matters and really matters more during dark times. We do know that hugs matter. We do know that money cannot drive away fear. We do know that our decision to plan our next moves were far more important than standing still in fear.

> What we do know is that being isolated is lonely. We do know that family matters and really matters more during dark times. We do know that hugs matter. We do know that money cannot drive away fear.

We were anchored by prayer and hope. We turned all our energy on seeing our sons and their families. We intentionally made some changes and we moved forward. Except for the videos of that night that are still on my phone. Should probably be deleted, right?

Acting In Faith

By Dr. Stacie NC Grant

"Acting in FAITH" is more than a trite saying or jargon. It is how we function when we don't understand what's going on around us. COVID-19 created the perfect storm of confusion globally. We didn't understand what we were witnessing. There was so much happening simultaneously, and the future was filled with so many unknowns. I realized that I could not act like the pandemic wasn't happening in real-time, but I was determined to keep acting in FAITH.

FAITH was my anchor and fueled my actions. My advice to my community of Faithpreneurs® (faith-based entrepreneurs and professionals) was to *"acknowledge what you see, but trust what you know."* Acknowledge that we are witnessing the traumatic loss of life in record numbers. Acknowledge that racial unrest hit a fever pitch that boiled over onto the streets, sparked by the murder of George Floyd. Acknowledge that financial insecurity was at an all-time high. Acknowledge that businesses were closing in high numbers. However, TRUST what you KNOW! What you know is trouble doesn't last always! What you know is if you believe with your free will that God is real and His Word is true and that He's the same God of yesterday, today, and tomorrow, then He will bring us through this. What you know is this is not our first rodeo with trial, tribulation, aggravation, and difficulty. We know that through every adversity there is opportunity.

When you trust what you know, it gives you the strength to pause and settle in the knowing that you are not in control. We can choose to honor the lives that have transitioned by how we live. That was how I was able to reconcile losing loved ones, extended family, and friends because the volume of loss was becoming overwhelming at times. It felt like I didn't have time to catch my breath between funeral programs. As I acted in FAITH, I also reconciled that all of what I was witnessing was God allowed or God-ordained.

> Little did I know that I would be tested by my own words when it hit home and shook the foundation of my FAITH. The uninvited guest of COVID-19 visited my family.

Little did I know that I would be tested by my own words when it hit home and shook the foundation of my FAITH. The uninvited guest of COVID-19 visited my family. My mother didn't realize that she was exposed to someone who tested positive for COVID-19. Initially, she simply was not feeling well, then one day she passed out. With the reality that all hospitals were filled with COVID cases, she was reluctant to go to the hospital. How grateful I am for my girlfriend who is a physician, taking time to provide telehealth support, while in the midst of caring for patients at a local hospital. She urged me to get Mom to urgent care for x-rays. It was there that spots of pneumonia were found on her lungs. There was no COVID-19 diagnosis however because they had run out of tests. They sent us home with medication to address the pneumonia.

COVID was the ugly elephant in the room that no one wanted to mention, even though we were all thinking it. My girlfriend continued to instruct me on what I needed to watch for. She started to deteriorate in her ability to move, desire to eat, or even read. I was experiencing firsthand the impact of this deadly virus. If my mother wasn't healthy before and had not taken good reasonable care of herself, I see how this strain of the coronavirus could have killed her. Therefore, but for the grace of God, we did not have to hospitalize her.

I stopped everything and started ACTING in FAITH! I took care of her around the clock as if I had a newborn baby, every four hours checking her breathing, giving her medication, making sure she had sufficient liquids in her; propping her up because we didn't want to lay her down. She took 5 to 10 minutes just to raise her head. That's how much the virus drains the life out of you. It attacks your ability to even want to breathe and move. This thing is like a demon, trying to suck the life out of people. I had to nurse my mom back to health. It took over two and a half months of me going back and forth between two households to make sure my family was okay and return to take care of her.

> I kept ACTING in FAITH, constantly reflecting on the fact that FAITH does not mean you're exempt from the trials and tribulations of life.

I cannot even begin to explain how I didn't end up COVID positive myself because I didn't care about myself at that point. It was my mother's life we were fighting for. There was nothing that I would not have done to make sure that she was okay. We didn't even have masks on in the house. I physically carried her to the bathroom as she propped herself against me. It took us 15 minutes to walk two yards to the bathroom. This was something

I wish on no one, but despite it all, I continued ACTING IN FAITH!

Even in the midst, I thanked God that I had the capacity to set my own schedule. I was grateful that I could stop everything to care for and nurse my mother back to health. I still managed a few meetings and even coordinated outreach for other senior citizens in my community who didn't have family nearby. I don't even know how I was functioning. I was on autopilot and would only sleep for a couple of hours each night. I had to check her breathing and every symptom that my friend told me to watch out for so that she would not end up in the hospital on a ventilator. Praise God for her full and complete recovery.

Without my faith and knowing that God was caring for and protecting me, there's no way I would be sharing this story today. I kept ACTING in FAITH, constantly reflecting on the fact that FAITH does not mean you're exempt from the trials and tribulations of life. FAITH does not mean that you won't contract COVID or know someone who has it or succumbed to it. What FAITH does is tell you whatever your portion is, God will sustain you through it. And your testimony becomes fuel for somebody else on their FAITH walk. The coronavirus pandemic that began invading lives in 2019 will be a part of the history books. Knowing that we will emerge on the other side of this trauma, we can choose to honor the thousands of lives who have transitioned with our contribution to the world. We can choose to live our lives by ACTING IN FAITH! Simply put – don't give up.

It has been said that when America catches a cold, black people get pneumonia! We've seen what underlying conditions can do if we don't take care of ourselves. We must increase our fight against high cholesterol, diabetes, obesity, stress, and other silent killers. Without fortifying your immune system and general health, you won't have the physical ability to fight this virus. We don't know what the next wave, the Delta variant, or other things that are coming up will do. But what we can do is learn from the pain and crisis that has already manifested. There's an opportunity for us to come out better, to come out stronger, to come out more resilient, to come out more aware of how we must take care of ourselves. We need to continue to boost our immune system and avoid getting caught up with conspiracy theories and false narratives. There is no one on this planet who has not been affected in some capacity by COVID-19 directly or indirectly so use wisdom in how you choose to operate. ACTING IN FAITH prompts you to take inspired action.

I gain strength from the following scripture *"Now faith is the substance of things hoped for, the evidence of things not seen"* (Hebrews 11:1, KJV). Thus, ACTING IN FAITH requires me to keep moving despite what it looks like. My FAITH doesn't tell me challenges won't happen. On the contrary, it prepares me to hold on to an anchor that won't allow me to sink while the storm is passing over!

> My FAITH doesn't tell me challenges won't happen. On the contrary, it prepares me to hold on to an anchor that won't allow me to sink while the storm is passing over!

Stay encouraged, use wisdom and consider ACTING in FAITH as you navigate this journey called life. Opportunity is typically on the heels of crisis, so get in position for the opportunities ahead for you. We cannot control everything, but we can control our ACTIONS! I am just asking you to consider anchoring your ACTIONS in FAITH!

An Unexpected Visitor

By Helen Hope Kimbrough

There was exhilaration and excitement as the countdown and ball drop on New Year's Eve 2019 led into the first day of 2020. Watch Night church services in churches and New Year's Eve parties were on blast. And this was not only going to be a new year, but a new decade to pursue goals and fulfill dreams more expansively. Things were going to be different in this new season. Yet, I could not imagine how different.

In January/February 2020, the world started receiving international and national reports of a deadly strain of the coronavirus. These reports intensified rapidly with thousands exposed or dying daily. Never in my wildest dreams would I have imagined this. Things would never be the same again. As of August 16, 2021, the *worldodmeters.info* reports that there have been 37, 469,989 coronavirus cases; 637, 572 deaths; and 30, 155, 008 who have recovered.

My journey during the COVID-19 pandemic and social unrest unfolded in an array of events that continue to take shape. These events encapsulate true stories that hopefully will resonate with you.

My Last In-Person Event

As a children's author, my last in-person event would take place at the Charlotte Convention Center on February 29, 2020. I partnered with Novant Health and the Collegiate International Athletic Association (CIAA) Fan Fest for a book reading and signing geared toward the importance of literacy in young readers. The energy that day was magnetic and captivating, and children and families were engaged with various author events and activities.

During these trying times, I stressed the importance of family, faith, and fortitude and how God's blessings were still shining upon us as a family. My goal was to keep them engaged, encouraged, and motivated.

When I look back on that day, I had a volunteer assigned to me to help make certain that everything flowed accordingly. After each reading segment, she cleaned profusely and kept germs at bay. I thanked her then for taking the time to keep everything sanitized. Today, I still thank her for the heightened awareness that she took in terms of safety for me, and the families represented there.

Schools Closed

By March 13, 2020, schools officially closed for in-person instruction. Colleges and universities also closed to keep students safe. We thought that schools would reopen within four to six weeks. We were totally wrong!

2020 Graduates

During the pandemic, I had two 2020 graduates. A senior in college and a senior in high school. Both worked hard on their academic standing to enjoy their respective senior years. However, they were thrust into completing their coursework online to graduate. Neither of them was pleased with the decision to close because they were literally going to have to complete their senior year at home and not be able to enjoy the full festivities that special time offers like prom, senior skip day, senior parties and trips, sports recognitions and the long-awaited reward of graduation ceremonies. During these trying times, I stressed the importance of family, faith, and fortitude and how God's blessings were still shining upon us as a family. My goal was to keep them engaged, encouraged, and motivated (with laughs, walks, talks, hikes, and board games, etc.). They truly pulled it together and both graduated with honors. A degree was mailed to my college graduate. There was no other fanfare but the celebratory moments on Zoom with family. My high school graduate did take part in an outdoor graduation ceremony allowing some milestone closure before entering the military academy.

Black Lives Matter

We love our brown and black sons and daughters, and we want them to survive, thrive, and prosper. They are worthy of all that God has created them to be.

It is hard to fathom the depth of institutional racism and unnecessary force that is used to kill, subdue, or ostracize people of color while driving a car, walking or running in a neighborhood, kneeling on a football field, waving a toy gun, whistling at a white woman, etc. Since the days of slavery, the violence that our ancestors endured is still playing out in real-time with people continuing to question why Black Lives Matter. The answer is simple. Because they do!

May 8, 2020, was an emotional day for me. It was a day that I joined the 2.23 Mile Dedication Distance Run to remember Ahmaud Arbery with my older son. Once again, I had to talk about unfair treatment and brutal injustices that led a young man to DIE for simply running and minding his own business. Arberry's death did not receive national attention until a video surfaced months later. He was actually killed on February 23, 2020.

Thereafter, Breonna Taylor was fatally shot in her home by police officers during a botched raid on March 13, 2020. No evidence of her involvement was found during the drug-related investigation. Her death was another instance of life gone too soon under the realm of faulty policing and police brutality.

Then, George Floyd's murder on May 25, 2020, at the hands of a corrupt police officer with three additional officers standing nearby was too much to take. Officer Derek Chauvin pressed his knee on Floyd's neck constricting his breathing for eight minutes and forty-six seconds without care for Floyd's humanity. On June 7, 2020, my family and I lit a candle and knelt for 8 minutes and 46 seconds. We reflected on his final words and last moments of life. [The trial of Derek Chauvin later proved that the time was longer — nine and a half minutes long.]

The torture and callousness of Floyd's death in particular and numerous killings of young men and women, and in some cases boys and girls, were unbearable and resulted in months of protests in the United States and abroad. I was compelled to protest and use my voice to speak against systemic racism and injustice and to shout to the world that BLACK LIVES MATTER.

Business Boomed!

Once the pandemic was underway, I was prepared to close shop and to minimally work on book projects. However, the opposite occurred. There was enormous interest in publishing books, and people were ready to share their stories without the cost being a factor. In my more than 15-year publishing career, 2020 was the BEST year in terms of book production, coaching clients, and offering webinars for emerging writers.

So why the change?

Many of my clients dreamed of writing their own book, and 2020 seemed like the perfect time to pursue something that they always wanted to do. Plus, with the shelter-in-place mandates and limited activities and travel outside of the home, folks hunkered down and started writing to make their dreams come true.

Likewise, there was a war cry to provide more diverse books and uncover disparities as it related to children's books. Therefore, I created workshops on "Why Race and Culture Matter to Storytelling and Diverse Children's Books" and "The Demand for More" as a way

> I was compelled to protest and use my voice to speak against systemic racism and injustice and to shout to the world that BLACK LIVES MATTER.

to delve into the importance of representation, inclusion, and unique experiences. It was apparent that it was time to change the narrative, and people embraced it.

Grandma Z

My grandmother was born in 1911 and experienced The Great Depression that took place from August 1929 – March 1933. During this time, there was a decrease in consumer spending and an increase in unemployment. Thankfully, my grandmother was resourceful and grew her own food, sewed her own clothes, and knew how to make a dollar stretch for her family beyond those turbulent times. She passed away in 2005.

Grandma Z became my unexpected visitor at the beginning of the pandemic. It was like she wanted to prepare me and walk me through a process of survival. She revealed so many things during this time, but this is what stands out:

- **Be prepared and spend wisely.** The pandemic will last longer than you think.

- **Be mindful.** The pandemic is like, yet different from The Great Depression.

- **Shop wisely.** Be wise about how you purchase food and supplies, and how often. [Based on this advice, I had a regimen of going to the grocery store every three weeks.]

- **Prepare your family.** Have a meeting with your family about food intake and how much they consume. Let them know that food will be there, but they may not always have their favorite things to eat.

- **Stay connected.** Faith, family, and friends will make you strong during uncertainty.

- **Remain calm.** Your family will respond to this situation based on how you respond to it. They are watching you.

- **Read and learn.** Continue to learn something new every day and be excited about it.

- **Go outside and get some fresh air.** Exercise individually or with your family. This is a great time of peace for you and bonding time with your family.

Grandma Z's voice spoke to me for months. I stopped hearing her voice - I guess - once she felt comfortable that I was staying on course. I am grateful for her instructions and lessons. Her insight kept my family sane and whole.

From previous years of lack and survival with my family as motivation, I walked by faith and not by sight.

What I Learned...

Although there are countless stories where people struggled during this season, I grew in comforting and immeasurable ways. From previous years of lack and survival with my family as motivation, I walked by faith and not by sight.

Only God got me through those years of hardship, uncertainty, and pain. With that muscle memory, my mind, body, heart, and soul were ready to tackle this new challenge with God as my fortress and strength and with Grandma Z whispering in my ear.

Today, I am filled with gratitude, hope, and praise believing that we can overcome anything together.

What I learned for sure is that I love being an introvert, meditating and having devotional time, working from home, experiencing things with child-like wonder, exercising and eating healthy, reading (I created a book club!), and singing, dancing, and talking on the phone (my favorite pastime). I've also learned that it is okay to embark upon bodacious goals as scary as that may be.

One Moment In Time

The Clear Assignment...Letting Pain Expose Your Purpose

By Gigi Gilliard

The early days of the arrival of COVID-19 were like scenes of a futuristic horror movie. However, one dreadful day brought us a trauma too unspeakable to be believed. It was a day involving three beloved family members—two of whom helped shape my early life; all fiercely loved.

In the late 1960s my parents were a young Black couple from the deep south, living in New York City and raising a baby for the first time. New to the big city, they found themselves in need of family help. My dad had an older aunt, who was already living in Harlem, raising her five young-adult aged kids. He and my mom asked my grand aunt if she would be willing to keep me while they worked. Her eldest girls, Janie and Susie, oversaw taking care of me. Without question the two of them helped build the foundation for my earliest years.

Equally instrumental to that early foundation was my Uncle Bobby, my mother's brother who had also moved to New York City from South Carolina. He lived with us shortly before I moved back to the Bronx from Harlem to live with my parents full-time. He became my full-time babysitter and my first best friend. Shortly after coming to New York, my uncle met his first love—my aunt Vivian Theresa—*"the prettiest girl riding a NYC subway train"*—he would say. Not long after first spotting her, he realized that they both worked in the same building. It wouldn't be long before they began dating and were married with a family reception in our backyard three years later in 1974.

While I certainly worried about my entire family, as COVID struck I had dire concern for Cousin Janie. At 73, (and diagnosed with colon cancer in 2015), she was at increased risk. Only venturing out for doctor and chemotherapy visits, she had a home health aide who visited daily to administer care. She was certainly at risk of exposure by the in and out visits.

He told me that he was not feeling well and reported he had felt unwell all day. Simultaneously, I could hear Auntie releasing a ghastly cough.

Uncle Bobby and Aunt Theresa, also both in their 70s, with underlying health conditions, were also greatly at risk. There was cause for alarm one Saturday in early March of 2020 when Uncle Bobby did not show for an important family affair. I called him and he told me that he was not feeling well and reported he had felt unwell all day. Simultaneously, I could hear Auntie releasing a ghastly cough. Frightened, I asked, "Uncle is it possible that you and Aunt T could have been exposed to COVID?" Initially he balked and said, "no way." He quickly remembered however, that Aunt Theresa did go to church the previous Sunday. He shared that her pastor called saying that someone at church had been exposed to COVID, and the congregation was being urged to get tested. By this time, COVID's spread dominated every news cycle. With each passing day, the threat of this lethal plague grew. COVID came with a terrible death sentence and with terrible terror.

In coming days, Uncle's fatigue was followed by a temperature, and the same horrendous cough I heard from my aunt. We urged them to seek medical care. Older, Black New Yorkers were skeptical of healthcare across the city as news outlets reported that thousands of COVID-stricken New Yorkers were dying in hospital hallways. However, on March 27, 2020, our pretty girl from the train began to have serious trouble breathing. There was no choice but to get Aunt Theresa in an ambulance and to a hospital.

In a daily group text thread, our family had been speaking openly about COVID-19 and our fears. My cousin shared, that like Aunt Theresa, her mother also had a terrible persistent cough along with other symptoms. With her mother reticent to go to the hospital, my cousin and her siblings eventually *forced* their mom to do just that. Once there, she was placed on a ventilator as was the practice for those struggling with the worse COVID symptoms. As our experiences converged, it happened that on March 27 of 2020 (when Aunt T was admitted to the hospital), my cousin's mother was removed from the ventilator as her condition improved. We were elated and we praised God!

In the wee hours of Sunday, March 29th however, sorrow swallowed our joy.

At 2:15 A.M., my sister gently woke me up, with obvious pain in her voice, to say that our beloved Cousin Janie had declined swiftly and had passed away an hour before. My first mentor, my first big sister, the pretty nurse who saw into my soul—was gone. I rolled out of bed onto the floor on my knees where I prayed and wept. With a heavy heart, I eventually got back in bed. I woke again when my sister returned to say that my dear Soror was on the phone to tell me that my cousin (also my Soror), had called to say that her mother did not make it! How? She was improving and had been removed from the ventilator! I called my cousin's home to speak with her. Her husband (also my fraternity brother) refused to put her on the phone saying, "she just cannot talk, Gi." How could it be that Cousin Janie and Cousin Sarah left us on the same day? I got back on my knees and tried to pray. Deep, repeated sobs of, "how, how can this be?" were all I could manage.

But as my tears streamed, the phone rang yet again. I strained to hear as my mother's voice was low and tight. She was speaking to my Uncle Bobby saying tersely, "Bob, this is not true. This cannot be true. Do nothing until we arrive." Unfathomable, but the hospital had called to say that our sweet Aunt Theresa had too lost her battle with COVID-19 just moments before.

March 29th, 2020, and three family members were gone from COVID, or complications thereof, on the same day. All before Noon. How on Earth could this be? Nothing was right and EVERY.SINGLE.THING.WAS.WRONG. In every cell of my body, I felt wretched despair. Despondency and unspeakable grief washed over me like an ocean wave, and I was drowning.

As I rushed to get dressed so that we could meet Uncle Bobby at the hospital (careful to stay more than six feet from him as he was indeed infected with COVID) I moved some papers around my desk. As I did so, my hand happened to pick up the last birthday card I had received from Cousin Janie. She wrote me often in her handwriting – especially after her cancer diagnosis – ensuring that I would continue to hear her voice. In this card, she shared that she was aware of how sick she was and wanted me to be prepared. On the last line of the card she wrote, *"now little Gigi you know I love you – don't start crying…and be strong."* Somehow, Cousin Janie was still speaking directly to me. I do not believe that she was discouraging me from grieving; but I do believe that she was making clear my assignment. In the second that I eerily found that card, I had a mindset shift. Everything I had been taught about family, love and duty would come together in the awareness of my assignment. Gigi was up to bat. I had resources and knowledge and know-how and God was counting on me. My grief made me physically ill, and I felt ill-equipped, but I knew that *love* was capable. My love that burns for my family could be used as the very reservoir of my strength.

Love would be my weapon as I filled the assignment to serve my family. It would fuel me in the days to come. It would comfort me as I was asked to comfort others. Love would propel me as I stood outside of the funeral home after services for my cousin's mother and shouted at her, "God is with you! God is with you!" Love would sustain me through countless hours of fighting with the city of New York to get my auntie's remains and have her transported to her hometown in Virginia. Love would thrust me as I cut up pounds of vegetables to make my uncle soups and teas to irrigate his lungs, boost his immune system and will him to fight back against that hateful disease. Love was power and it gave me the strength of a thousand men as I moved on my assignment.

Finding our purpose and living for that purpose changes the game. The narrative becomes less about us, and more— about others.

COVID had stolen my people, but it could not—and would not—rob my love.

As we moved through the months since that terrible day, I have come to see the world differently. Everything is now divided into only two categories—does this *help* my purpose, or does it *hurt* it? Does this thought, action, plan, project, or person promote or obstruct my assignment?

Finding our purpose and *living for that purpose* changes the game. The narrative becomes less about us, and more—about others. HOW can we serve? WHERE can we serve? WHAT was I, *what were YOU*, brought to this Earth to do? There is an assignment that is just for you; an assignment that is just for me. Things that need fixing in this world that only YOUR unique efficacy can fix. Living in, and for, our purpose can bring healing, can bring comfort, can bring wholeness. Find that purpose, my sweet biscuits—and be clear about your assignment.

Missing the Healthy Me

By Marilyn Johnson

"Healthy Me" (or HM, as I now call my former self), slipped away from my grasp in 2020. She did not say a formal good-bye or leave me with a warm, endearing embrace. Though, to her credit, I must admit that she did give me warning signs that her departure was looming. The warning signs were disguised as headaches, muscle pains, and frequent imbalance but they were signs nonetheless that there was a problem in our relationship. Since she spent six decades gifting me a life of exercise and physical activity—I accepted her departure quietly. Should I have asked her more questions, probed more intently before she left? Perhaps.

HM excelled as an active tomboy. She was always playing organized sports in her neighborhood and throughout school. If it was competitive, she was there. If it was active, she was there. HM enjoyed the thrill of playing and all the games. Cheerleading, dance, gymnastics, Pilates are proof of her past achievements in physical excellence. She counted two safe and healthy pregnancies as celebratory achievements to her good health as well. HM's athletic skills did not go unnoticed, or undervalued. Competitive sports were the entre to practiced leadership, character development and dedicated discipline. Her confidence showed when she took any corporate or community stage. With fervor and energy, she could garner the attention and deliver a rousing presentation. Admittedly, I took the good health relationship I enjoyed with HM for granted.

HM and I lived life day to day, almost effortlessly enjoying the fulfilling experiences of seeing our childhood dreams come to life. Those night visions and daydreams were often of climbing the proverbial ladder of success, not just professionally, but socially and spiritually. Together, hand in hand, we grew, achieved, conquered our goals, inspired others, and enjoyed the life we were living. Along the journey, she pointed out to me from time to time, that she noticed relatives, grandparents, friends, and colleagues were traveling paths of maladies and sickness. It seemed that these health scares and challenges that life presents increased with each birthday. No one could escape them. But HM was healthy and because she was, I was as well.

> Together, hand in hand, we grew, achieved, conquered our goals, inspired others, and enjoyed the life we were living.

HM and I offered patience, compassion, consolation, and comfort to all those she knew who were struggling with disease or illness in their physical bodies. Some recovered, while others succumbed based on life's predetermined timeline. Yet, when Mother Nature had the upper hand, she accepted their fate with nonchalance and the understanding that to everything there is a season.

Then, it happened. HM began to notice health deterioration both physically and mentally in early 2020. The more she noticed it and screamed warnings to me, the more I noticed it. Her gradual physical decline bid her farewell and there I was fully engaged in the loss of HM.

In an accelerated fashion during COVID-19, my life – now fully void of HM- took a drastic direction. Healthy Me serenely slipped away, and I noticed that there was no promise to return soon. I did not know if I would ever see her again and she gave me no clues. Healthy Me relented to a diagnosis of SVT (supraventricular tachycardia) or rapid heart rate and more symptoms described as "bradykinesia", or "slow movement of muscles". Healthy Me was now just me and a diagnosis that felt like it was designed to snatch all of our dreams, goals, and plans to conquer so much.

> The social isolation of COVID-19 was a prism of reflection, rather than a prison of unhealthy fear. Every day was repetitious yet unfamiliar as I socially distanced.

The social isolation of COVID-19 was a prism of reflection, rather than a prison of unhealthy fear. Every day was repetitious yet unfamiliar as I socially distanced. The parable we have all heard "…life is too short", rang loudly (and continues to echo often), as HM disappeared from the hospital room where she was admitted when her heart rate reached 168 bpm for over one hour. Yet, while in hospital, the drug Adenosine saved my life. Her heart was arrested to total quiet for several seconds, and then my heart restarted in its natural rhythm. Again, Mother Nature had the upper hand.

Over the following weeks and months, I would be faced with a slew of reactions and symptoms to the illness that overtook me. The muscular pain intensified, as did the headaches, there were sudden tremors, and other things; and I began to wonder if any part of HM would live through me. I still wonder the same thing. As a matter of fact, the tremors remain, the treatments continue, vascular bradykinesia was explored, medicines have been prescribed and administered, but HM is gone. Moreover, she is missed. Although treatable, the symptoms that I took on from her departure will require therapy, prescriptive medications, and supervised medical attention. Not just for a month or two, but forever. Forever, is in need of a long time to dwell in managed physical decline.

Avoiding COVID-19 continues to be a strategic health goal globally; my condition warranted that I take it on like a heavy-weight title match. Contracting a critical and potentially dead-line version of the coronavirus was not something I could add to my medical or self-care. Thus, both Pfizer vaccines were administered and every pandemic protocol that was recommended by health officials became part of my routine. I, the Less Healthy Me, adopted and share the mantra "listen to your heart" with everyone I meet. I share this mantra to encourage others to pay attention to cues and signs from your body that something is not right. That lingering headache could be a problem. Those sudden falls or trips from being imbalanced could be a problem. That unusual tingling in your arm and your chest could be a problem. The healthier you will tell you when there is something making you unhealthy. Listen to your heart. Listen to your body. Listen to that thing that something is wrong here.

While listening, you may hear the voice of a healthier version of yourself. You might notice that you are missing the tonal strength, the physical vitality, the harmonic clarity, that overall feeling of wellness, and the quick recall of facts and figures… that version of your health is begging for attention. Do not ignore the clues. I promise you will appreciate the audible reward of hearing your own beating heart.

Pursuing Peace

By Rev. Teraleen R. Campbell

Periods of Darkness

The time in which we are living has presented more challenges than most have encountered in our lifetimes. The past year and a half (2020-2021) has tested me in ways that I never imagined. I consider myself to be a positive, glass half full, extroverted introvert. I love people, but am an only child; therefore, I am also comfortable in my own space. Pre-pandemic, I was so busy that I had to build free weekends into my schedule in order to practice better self-care.

During the early part of the shutdown, I saw being at home as a blessing and an opportunity to rest from the rat race of life. I quickly realized that was not always the case. I work in the property management industry, although not front-line, it is considered essential work since we provide a necessity to the public. Additionally, being in ministry, the needs of those to whom I minister increased exponentially. The calls to speak with, pray for, and present to parishioners came week after week as people tried to make sense of what was happening and hold onto their faith.

I was blessed to transition from a company with rigid work conditions to work for a company that enabled me to predominantly work from home. However, I soon learned that working from home could yield longer hours than going into an office. I got into the habit of working 10 to 12-hour days at least four days per week. As I reflect, I think doing so was a coping mechanism after enduring months of quarantine. Working helped mask the feelings of isolation and loneliness that I began to experience. After all, I live alone and had not seen my family since December 2019. Due to the pandemic, I could no longer enjoy the fellowship of church, various events, movies, traveling, or outings with friends.

> I soon learned that working from home could yield longer hours than going into an office. I got into the habit of working 10 to 12-hour days at least four days per week.

The problem was those long work hours began to burn me out, whew! I found myself mentally exhausted, with no tangible outlet to soothe those feelings. On top of it, I felt as though I could not share my feelings with anyone because, hey, we are amid a pandemic, and everyone has their own crosses to bear. Besides, I am not one who tends to dump my issues on other people. Therefore, I dealt with it privately.

It Was Necessary

Although not under good circumstances, it is now apparent that we were all given a collective pause. Some have rejected it and become angry. Alas, I am clear that God makes no mistakes. Although we were caught off guard, He was not.

At the end of the day, this period of pause was mine to accept. I came to the realization that I had options: 1) either remain in the abyss of burnout, and feeling overwhelmed that God had previously delivered me from, 2) take back my time, even if it was time that would be spent at home, alone.

This pause came with a reminder. Here I was two years after being downsized from a company that I'd spent 26 years of my career with working excessive hours to be successful. At first, I did not mind and rationalized that I was in the comfort of my home. However, by the end of the summer, I was overwhelmed and feeling the effects of my brain being in work mode for most of my awake hours.

> I promised myself that I would not spend more time building someone else's legacy than I do my own. I had done that for 26 years and vowed not to allow history to repeat itself.

After my position had been eliminated by my former employer, I made myself a promise. I promised myself that I would not spend more time building someone else's legacy than I do my own. I had done that for 26 years and vowed not to allow history to repeat itself. The reality was that I had drunk that Kool-Aid, thinking that being an exceptional employee would lead to stability and eventually retirement. I learned that the Kool-Aid had turned bitter, and I did not recognize it.

I also gained the revelation that while I regularly prayed for countless others, I did not harness that same energy when it came to taking *my* burdens to the Lord. I could not continue in that manner. I did not want to lose *myself* again to a grind. I didn't know how long this pandemic would last, but I had to find my rhythm.

Seeing the Light

I took time to evaluate what building my legacy would consist of. I examined my personal passions and the assignments that God had given me. I evaluated where those assignments stood and identified steps to complete them.

Having done that, the first major step was to establish personal boundaries for the thing that caused me to burn out – work. I reminded myself that God has given me a purpose. Therefore, I cannot live to work, instead, I must work to live.

I set boundaries and timeframes to eliminate working excessively. I prayed and asked the Lord to show me suitable activities to engage in to combat feeling isolated. I set aside one day each week as *my self-care self-prayer day*. On that day, I pray specifically for myself, no one else. I cast my cares upon the Lord. I tell Him what I want, and talk about my dreams, goals, and challenges.

One very significant legacy building assignment came to me at the end of 2020, it was to establish a scholarship in memory of my beloved mother who passed away in 2017. My mom had me when she was single, although she later married and divorced. For years she mentored and provided tangible support to those whom she mentored. She also tried to complete her college degree, but life happened, and she was not able to complete her studies. To that end, the scholarship's target student is a single parent. I made provisions to cover the scholarship personally, but God being God did exceedingly and abundantly over what I could ask or think, and people donated toward the effort. I am excited to have awarded the scholarship to a wonderful applicant.

While you may not provide a scholarship, I encourage you to evaluate your passions and identify connections that will support building your legacy.

There was another key component to walking in purpose and passion. I had to learn how to give myself the same amount of grace that I had extended to others. I had to realize that I was living through an extended period of uncertainty, instability, darkness, and grief. When I sat and thought about it, I personally have lost numerous people in my life during the pandemic, with the most significant being my godmother (2020) and a close friend at the beginning of 2021. The losses were exasperated by not being able to have proper closure through traditional funerals. It was like salt in the wound of the grieving process. With that in mind, more grace is necessary. To some degree, establishing the Cindy Moses Memorial Scholarship allowed me to channel some of my grief in a positive direction while doing something that was within my control amid other losses where I was helpless.

Another passion is the work that I do to support caregivers. I recognize that this is one of my God-given assignments during this season. At the onset of the pandemic, I received calls and requests to aid in supporting people experiencing a different type of grief. Many caregivers were suddenly faced with working from home or not at all. Consequently, they have a family member with dementia or Alzheimer's in the home who sees them more often but does not understand the boundaries of telework. Unfortunately, they think that their daughter, son, husband, or wife is home so they can do whatever they ask them to do. Of course, we know that is not the case.

Pursuing my passions put me in a place of indescribable peace. I am reminded of Psalm 34:14, "Seek peace and work to maintain it."

Caregivers have also struggled with lockdowns and quarantines at the facilities where their loved ones reside. That takes a loved one outside of their routine which can cause more harm than good in the long run. Not being able to visit loved ones or accompany them to hospitals has wreaked havoc on many. Add to that the ultimate challenge – the death of someone that we could not say goodbye to.

Seeing the needs has made me passionate about being a tool to stand in the gap as it relates to helping caregivers in a variety of ways such as praying with them or sending encouraging messages or providing content in the form of webinars specifically to educate them.

Pursuing my passions put me in a place of indescribable peace. I am reminded of Psalm 34:14, *"Seek peace and work to maintain it."*

As you move through this season, I offer the following tips:

1. Align with like-minded people and disconnect from those who are not. One group will be passion pushers and the latter will be passion killers. Identify and disconnect accordingly.

2. Do not apologize for enforcing your personal boundaries.

3. Practice spiritual self-care. Feed your soul.

4. If you journal, review it periodically. Review your growth and progress.

5. Know that the light will shine in your life again.

Honor Thy Mother…

By Marie Turner McCleave

My mother was quickly succumbing to dementia and the family knew that it would be impossible to care for her in any of our homes. We decided that the best care for her would be in a community with constant care. So, fourteen years ago, we decided to place our 91-year-old mother in a nursing home in New Jersey. She was but a phone call away.

In the early stages of her memory challenges, she still knew me. During the later stages, I am thankful that I still knew her. I felt helpless because I live in and assist my husband with our family business in Georgia. The anxiety of not being able to see her more often was emotionally taxing. It became even more frustrating and concerning when all family visitation was canceled in March of 2020 as COVID protocols were established for nursing homes.

It was devastating news to hear that our country had been stricken with a deadly virus and at that time, there was no vaccine. There was also no comfort in the safety of travel for quick weekend visits to New Jersey. So, when I was notified that Mom had contracted the virus during the first week in April 2020, I was surprised and shocked. She had gone from no symptoms to a COVID-positive reality. I was angry because I could not see her.

During this time of uncertainty and anger, I received a phone call at 2:30 P.M. on April 18 from the sister of one of my life-long friends. Knowing that he was sick with a heart condition and cancer, I was still shocked and deeply saddened to hear that he had passed. Two hours later, one of my three sisters called to share the heart-wrenching news that our mother had passed.

I was already beside myself in tears and then to hear that my mother died within hours of my dear college classmate was over-whelming. What am I supposed to do without my mother? This incurable virus had killed her. I was angrier than ever before. The grief was crushing. Two people who I loved dearly - gone on the same day.

I had to renew my conversations with God and lean on my faith. But how would I rediscover my faith during the pandemic and a virus that had taken my mother?

I was also stressed because my family members each handled my mother's diagnosis and passing dif-ferently. This only added to a pe-riod of discord which introduced the added burden of the price of family love. It is steep. Forgiveness is even steeper. This part of my journey was extremely challenging. Yet, I had to accept the passing of my mother.

I had to renew my conversations with God and lean on my faith. But how would I rediscover my faith during the pandemic and a virus that had taken my mother? I depended as I always have on my trust and belief in God's Holy Word. I would continue to see light where darkness appeared. I would continue to motivate others as I practiced self-care. I would continue to be thankful for knowing what to do because I was taught how to be a survivor by my mother. I kept repeating the words that I had heard for four years during Vesper Services at Livingstone College, "No matter how dark the night, joy comes in the morning!"

When my dad was killed in an accident at 32, my 29-year-old mother was left to raise four girls, eight years old and under. My maternal grandmother offered to raise two of us. My mother said, "thanks, but no thanks." She profoundly and unequivocally declared that she would raise us together. She kept her word by slicing everything we had four ways. When my brother was born nine years later, life became a five-way split.

When I left New Jersey to attend Livingstone College in North Carolina, it was my first adventure beyond the family home. My one trunk was all I took with me. It had my best winter, summer, spring, and fall wardrobe items. I had learned that it did not take much to survive from my mother. She raised her family with grit and determination. She was a survivor and that is the legacy that she instilled in me that I continue to uphold.

It is the legacy that I now share with my three grandchildren. They lost their paternal grandmother on September 11, 2020, five months after my mother passed. My daughter, grandchildren, and I found ourselves once again relying on that survival trait when two of my three grandchildren could no longer attend school. My daughter and I began to home school the five and 13-year-old at the end of February 2020; with a six-month-old baby at home. I felt the fortitude of my mother's sustainable lessons as I engaged with helping to care for my grandchildren. Despite the constant pandemic disruptions, we walked out of the situation calling upon survivorship and sustainability as our anchors.

What I now know through this journey is that I will be reunited with my mother in God's time by leaning on my faith. It is that same faith in God, and the fire to survive that carries me through each day and can carry you through as well.

I Reduced the Noise and Emerged with a Baby During Chaos

By Tamara McGill McFarland

On January 23, 2020, while sitting in my OBGYN's office there was a recurring thought running through my mind. What was going to make this pregnancy different from those that previously ended in loss? I have come to terms with the fact that I have little to no control over what can happen within the first 12 weeks of gestation. I had become accustomed to hearing bad news at my 12-week appointments, however, I remained hopeful. During the ultrasound my doctor silently and diligently searched for my baby's heartbeat, once again it wasn't there. I prepared myself to console the women at the doctor's office as they tried to console me. Crazy right? I have been pregnant and had so many miscarriages that I was on a first-name basis with the staff at my doctor's office. I could feel them watching me and wanting to help me find comfort at the moment, but little did they know I was not going to allow myself to fall apart, to be weak, or seem helpless. My sentiment was I am a black woman in America, there is no room for weakness. I told everyone that everything was okay. I didn't even stop by the nurses' station for a grief counseling session; at this point, I could give the sessions.

I've always wanted to wait until I was older to have children. Many women are choosing to do the same; however, your plan and the plans of the universe may not be aligned. My husband and I began our pregnancy journey in our late thirties. We had a miscarriage, conceived naturally again, and then had our daughter. I wanted more than anything to give her a sibling that would be close in age. I have two bonus children from my husband's previous marriage, but they are adults and live outside of our home.

Now that we are in our forties, this was it! This was going to be our last time trying to expand our family. The pregnancy that I lost in January 2020 was through natural conception. I get pregnant easily, the issue has been carrying to full term. I know several women who have tried alternative methods to get pregnant and have been successful after many attempts. We decided to try in vitro fertilization (IVF). IVF assists with preventing genetic problems, fertilization, the progression of the embryo, and implantation to allow for conception in a controlled environment. It is one of the more widely known types of reproductive assistance. The likelihood of success depends on various factors, although IVF is scientific and controlled, it is not guaranteed. Having a healthy child is a miracle. We had tried IVF before, and it was unsuccessful; still, we agreed to try once more.

I had a five-year-old early riser who was the only child in the house. I had to become her teacher, new bestie, lab rat for her many experiments, and her partner in crime. She owned me!

March 2020 was the month that we decided to begin the IVF process; little did we know, the world was going to shut down and be forever changed during that time. The first weekend in March, a few days after my doctor's appointment my husband and I planned a trip to the Turks and Caicos Islands to relax and unwind before gearing up for my IVF cycle a few weeks later. The plan was to return home feeling renewed and ready to go. What did I say about plans and the universe?

We returned home on March 6 to news of COVID-19 running rampant through New York City. The following week we were on lockdown and practicing social distancing. Everything was surreal, I felt as if I were in a movie. The fertility clinic had stopped all cycles that had not begun before COVID.

I could not believe it, we had finally gotten to a place and space where we had a physician that we liked, a plan to move forward, and our world turned upside down. I did not want to try to get pregnant again naturally and risk another miscarriage. I had just lost a life, could not live my life, nor could I create life. Not to mention, I had a five-year-old early riser who was the only child in the house. I had to become her teacher, new bestie, lab rat for her many experiments, and her partner in crime. She owned me! I was exhausted. The days and times we're running together. We couldn't visit family and they couldn't visit us. I was annoyed with everyone that spoke as if this was some magical time to get organized or to start new businesses when I could barely get dressed for my day and draw on eyebrows! (Mama likes to be cute!) How could these people be doing so well when I was drowning? Was I ever going to be able to have another child? Was this it? Why universe? WHY? There was no end in sight to the madness.

No one knew how long this pandemic was going to last. It was time to focus on feeding my soul. I also had to come to terms with the fact that maybe I wasn't going to physically have another child. The possibility of adoption remained on the table.

I couldn't control what was happening around me and as a true control freak, the pandemic was bothersome. I had been telling myself that I was going to get into better shape and a better place spiritually before the pandemic and decided to resume meditation and yoga. I found a good meditation app, a few YouTube workout videos, and I focused on the world around me that I could control. I wasn't thinking about what everyone else was doing and what was working for them. I had to block out the noise; understanding that, sometimes people say things to others to motivate themselves. I could not take that on personally. I had to make sure that I was taking care of my mental health, and my family.

After a month or so I grew tired of being in emotional limbo. In the words of one of my favorite books written by Spiritual Leader and Author Iyanla Vanzant, *One Day My Soul Opened Up*! I made a conscious decision to make time for myself by getting up early to put myself first. I did not want to walk out of this pandemic looking like I had been through a pandemic!

I'm not a fitness guru, I'm not a super fit person, however, it makes me feel good to work out. I decided, why not get fit, mind, body, and soul. While I'm waiting for this thing to work itself out, I'm not going to sit and wallow in uncertainty. I'm going to be ready when the opportunity presents itself to try to grow my family. I am a black woman in America and a queen. And as a friend shared with me one day, queens do not run their countries by happenstance, they run them with grace.

I gave myself a purpose and a goal - take the best care of myself. I woke up at five A.M. before my little early riser, while the house was peaceful and still. I would sit in my thoughts, meditate, and work out Monday through Friday. I began to feel at peace, I had more patience for my husband and my little one. I found a space in the madness that allowed me to reconnect with myself in a way that would not have happened if the world did not stop.

Around August 2020, as our country adjusted to the pandemic and some businesses were reopening slowly with mask mandates, the fertility clinic began to resume treatments. We received a phone call asking if we wanted to move forward with the IVF process. I didn't know what was going to happen. I knew that by changing my mindset, finding peace, and staying fit that it was now or never!

The first seven days of IVF treatments are crucial. If your embryo survives within the first seven days and your chromosomes are balanced, you can move forward. I was at peace, so we moved forward. I felt positive about the process and the procedure went smoothly. Due to the pandemic, my husband was not allowed to accompany me into the facility, but no worries, I adjusted my crown and walked in.

I became pregnant from the procedure, and 12 weeks later it was time for a visit to my OBGYN to hear the baby's heartbeat for a confirmation of life. I was calm, yet anxious. This was my last ride in the maternity rodeo. The ultrasound technician began the process and there was our baby's heartbeat! It was beating strong and healthy, I sobbed! After everything that we had been through, in the middle of a world surrounded by chaos, in my mid-forties, I was finally having another baby!

> Figure out what moves you, what matters, and seriously ponder what were you working toward before the outside noise became a loud interruption.

I quarantined, meditated, worked out, did yoga, I was in a happy cocoon. On May 14, 2021, we welcomed our handsome little boy home. He is the most resilient amazing little being and a joy. We are happy and blessed beyond measure.

During times of chaos and uncertainty in your life, find your center, be still, find peace. Figure out what moves you, what matters, and seriously ponder what were you working toward before the outside noise became a loud interruption. Hold on to that and move forward. You got this, adjust your crown, and rule your kingdom.

We Wear The Mask

I Can't Fake it Anymore

By Natasha Sunday Clarke

Ring…ring…ring. It was January 27th, and I could hear the sound of my phone ringing. But how could this be? I always kept my phone on vibrate. Ring…ring…ring. Here I was, lying on the floor, wondering, am I really doing this? What is going on with me? Ring…ring…ring. What will they say? Ring…ring…ring. This is so embarrassing. Ring…ring…ring. I can't keep doing this. Ring…ring…ring. I am tired of pretending. Ring…ring…ring. I am not as strong as everyone wants me to be. Ring…ring…ring. I want to rest. Ring…ring…ring. "Hello, where are you? Are you okay?" That's all I heard on the other line. My response was simple, "I can't fake it anymore."

I guess you can say I have always been this way, an extrovert to most, one who can adapt to any situation. At least that is what I have allowed others to see and believe. Deep down, I am extremely shy. I prefer not to be in large crowds and I still get nervous when I am asked to speak publicly. Yet, when the lights come on and the cameras are rolling, it's show time. I smile and laugh when people say, "wow, you are a natural"; but in my head,

I want to tell them, I'm not a natural and I'm tired of smiling. But I can't do that, what will people say?

For over 20 years, I have served my country honorably. Three combat tours, three overseas assignments, and I have been afforded the opportunity to work for and with some outstanding people. The United States Army is all I know. Anyone who truly knows me, will tell you that my entire world has always revolved around the Army; and that's not a cliché. I have put the Army before everyone and everything. I didn't realize how institutionalized I had become. Mentally I had fixated my mind on a mark that would place me in life or death situation—literally.

> I have put the Army before everyone and everything. I didn't realize how institutionalized I had become. Mentally I fixed my mind on the mark that would place me in life-or-death situations—literally.

Stress, depression, and anxiety were words that I have heard for years, but seemed to ignore the signs when it came to my own mental health. Maybe it started in 2003 during my first deployment when I began to have sharp chest pains. They would come and go. I ignored the signs, but soon the pain would increase, so I decided it was time for me to seek medical attention. Anxiety is what the doctors said I was experiencing. I was prescribed medicine that would help calm my nerves whenever I would feel anxious. As the years went on, I found myself competing against this "fictitious" career clock. A metaphoric clock created several decades ago by a young, impressionable, full-time student athlete and Senior Reserve Officer Training Corps cadet who had her eyes set on becoming the second African American female General Officer to graduate from a prestigious university. I had to prove to everyone that I could accomplish any task or goal, regardless of how I was feeling physically or mentally. Besides, what will people think?

The standards of mediocracy no longer applied to me. I began to change from being happy-go-lucky, to becoming more focused, determined and institutionalized. I began to live and operate in a constant state of stress. I no longer had an off button. I was always on—24-hours a day, seven days a week. I was going to be NUMBER ONE, by any means necessary.

With military service in the top spot in my life, the placement of other relationships was questionable. Initially, I did not really want a family. In my mind, having a family would slow me down from being selected for top-tier military assignments. I had not figured out the perfect time to be a wife or parent. And even after I was blessed with a husband and children, I still chose the military over them. As stressful as it was, I chose the assignments that required me to be away for days and months on end. I even said yes, to the multiple senior-level executive jobs. If it meant I was going to reach my goal, I was going to say yes.

My physical health began to decline. After the chest pains, soon came the migraines, a slipped disk in my back due to nerve damage, and finally multiple blood clots which ultimately left me unable to have any more children. One would think that these would be signs for me to slow down, unfortunately, this was the start of my denial and self-medicating. I continued to ignore the signs of my body until it was almost too late.

Here I was, still chasing this imaginary clock of this college student, instead of facing the reality of life in front of me. I wanted to make everyone proud, I had to make everyone proud. No one from the military knew about all my medical ailments. There was no way I was going on medical profile; I faked my way through any type of rigorous and physical training by increasing my medication to numb the pain. I had mentally convinced myself and everyone around me – including my family and closest friends— that I had it all together. I was good at playing the game. There was no way I was going to give up, I had come too far. Besides, what will people think?

It wasn't just the military where I could not say no. I joined a sorority and I devoted numerous hours to my sisterhood. I didn't want to let anyone down. People depended on me, they knew my work ethic, and they understood that I always delivered and that I would always get the job done. Then there was my mentorship organization. Even though the meetings didn't require much, I was needed for the phone calls, emails, counseling, and mentorship. My soldiers, mentees, sorors, and friends needed me. Yes, it was tiring and stressful, but they needed me to help get them through their circumstances or help solve their problems. I was the go-to, or at least that is what people labeled me. I took on that title. I was the shero or the GOAT to many. It always seemed like my days were running together or as if I was running up against the clock. I never stopped and continued to push myself just a little harder. I never wanted to let anyone down. At some point, I should have sought counseling, but I was afraid. What would people think? No one would want to talk to me if they knew I was seeing a mental health provider. I buried my emotions and cried often when I was alone. Yet, I put up a good face to keep others from trying to see through me.

My spiritual life unfolded. Yet, I couldn't seem to set aside time to focus on my spiritual readiness. Physically I was showing up for church, but mentally, my mind was working overtime. I prayed, but most certainly not the way I should have or the way I knew how. Mostly because I was ashamed and afraid of my own actions. For almost 20 years, I had mastered this poker face. I never reached out to anyone to help me. What would I say? How would they perceive me? True, my spirit may have been dying on the inside, but I was still able to push through on the outside because I felt as though people still genuinely needed me. I continued to devote what little time I had left to everyone but myself. I faked my way through by quoting scriptures, sending encouraging words and smiling though my pain.

My family and I were stationed outside the U.S. when the global wide pandemic of COVID-19 plagued our nation. Unequivocally, 2020 fostered extremism, sexism, police brutality, and the injustices of racial inequality. Those same incidents that sparked so much in our country, infiltrated the military ranks. It hurt, as I watched my first love—the military—divide along racial and cultural lines. My mind could not process what was happening.

In the same year, I received an evaluation that was not good, and it broke me. I isolated myself and grew numb. I no longer wanted to play the game. I was wrestling with thoughts of suicide. I never thought I would contemplate ending my life. How selfish of me! But I was hurting. The anxiety, depression and crying myself to sleep at night overshadowed my mind and my thoughts. Professionally and mentally, I had hit rock bottom, my clock stopped. Instead of helping people, I felt as though the same people and the organizations I belonged to were using me. It was as if my mind was playing tricks on me. I began to wear my emotions on my sleeve and those emotions began to creep into my home.

> I wanted to change, but it was too late, I didn't know how. I had been living the superwoman image for so long.

I wanted to change, but it was too late, I didn't know how. I had been living the superwoman image for so long. Each time I attempted to reach out to a mental health provider, my pride got in the way. I believed that those in my circles saw my life as picture perfect.

Ring…ring…ring. I was curled at the foot of my bed as I held the phone to my ear. On January 27, 2021, I was popping pills and washing them down with alcohol. Since I had been self-medicating over the years, my tolerance level was extremely high. Naturally, I thought that was the reason it was taking so long for the pain to stop. Ring…ring…ring. I answered the phone, besides, at this point, it was too late…or so I thought. It was my best friend. God had sent my ram in the bush. "No matter what" is what we would say to one another in challenging times. That was the posture she took to help save me. No matter what. She was there to see me through that night. What if I had decided to give up? What if I decided not to answer the phone? What would people have said?

It's interesting how a circumstance or event (job loss, debt, bad relationship, poor health, suicide), can change an entire life. I try not to dwell on the past; however, I do use the night of January 27th as a reminder to live and not get bogged down or fixated on my childhood clock. There will be many who will say what about your family as a reason to live? If you have never been in the situation, if you have never been depressed or stressed, know that telling a person what they should or should not be thinking does not help. The best thing to do is to seek help immediately. Don't brush off the signs thinking a person is seeking attention. Sometimes the attention is a cry for help.

This journey to mental stability has been tough because I am very private and still a little prideful. Most days for me are better than the rest. I still have my doubts. Questioning my decision about my mental and physical health based on triggers that arise from certain events or circumstances. My mind still wanders to the assumed ridicule or judgment of what others may think of me. I had to accept the fact that behavioral health is not bad. I was and am not alone. There were others around me facing some of the same issues, including thoughts and even attempts of suicide.

As I continue to move through this journey of improved mental health, I'll dig deeper – when I'm ready – and face other issues that have spanned over 20 years. As I become more comfortable and less vulnerable, I will open up and communicate more. I no longer put on a different face or fake it per se. I am mentally free to be authentically me. On January 31, 2021, God gave me my purpose and I thank Him every day for my second chance at life.

My Freshman Year of College

By Audrey Washington

When looking back at my freshman year in college, I feel accomplished but also disappointed. Accomplished, because academically I made the Dean's List. I maintained a good grade point average, and I clearly did not fail any of my classes. I was disappointed because my first year was in the middle of a deadly pandemic. I did not experience all the things you prepare youself for or you hear people talk about like freshman orientation, in-person classes, in-person school events, or witness firsthand the friendly smiles from students and faculty. It was difficult to make friends because most of my classes were online. Instead of being in a classroom, I was confined to my dorm room, alone. I could not even make friends with my assigned roommate since she left at the beginning of the school year. Many weren't ready for pandemic college days.

Even with these obstacles I was determined to make the best of my long-awaited freshman school year in college. During the accomplishments and disappointments, I was confronted with reminders that my mental health struggles were still around. It was a silent battle that I had waged through my development years.

Being alone for large chunks of time and stuck in my room most of the time, my mental health was getting worse. I knew I could not go on in a dark place, therefore I decided to seek help. I was always scared to get help; my feelings were not validated for so long. Still, I knew I had to take matters into my own hands. I reached out to the resources on campus. Not only was I able to receive counseling services, but I was able to express myself freely and get the validation I had been wanting. I was finally told that what I was feeling was real and that I was not being dramatic or emotional. I was told that it would be okay.

Seek help, do not be concerned with what anyone may think or with anyone else's opinion of what getting counseling means. Be open, honest and vulnerable with your counselor; your transparency will help them identify the right tools and practices to assist you.

The professional help I got made a difference in my life so that I was able to continue experiencing my first year of college in a healthier way—mentally and emotionally, outside of the pandemic. I went outside more. I ate better. Overall, I felt better, all because I overcame my fears and got help.

I do believe I achieved a lot in my first year as a college student. I did have to go through my first year as a college student in the middle of a pandemic and I was already nervous about going into a whole new environment. Yet, I am so encouraged to know that if I handled my freshman year of college in a pandemic and with a global shutdown, I can handle whatever the future throws at me.

College presents many challenges. Course loads, professor requirements, balancing a social life with academic studies, making good grades, internships and in some cases working. Add to that mix COVID-19 which drastically and negatively affects personal interaction, arguments about masks, heated chats about vaccines, and things become overwhelming. Seek help, do not be concerned with what anyone may think or with anyone else's opinion of what getting counseling means. Be open, honest and vulnerable with your counselor; your transparency will help them identify the right tools and practices to assist you. Stay away from environments and people who increase your anxiety, depression, suicidal thoughts, thoughts of failure or who consistently disrespect and reject you. Find emotionally and mentally healthy people to hang out with. Even in a pandemic they exist on college campuses.

Whatever your counselor recommends as a tool for you, participate in it. You have to be your biggest support. Stay excited—the Dean's List, graduation and the career you are studying for are yours to achieve. I am excited about my continuing college journey and determined to succeed academically and emotionally. I will be able to attend a normal schedule of in-person classes; I will attend my weekly therapy sessions; I will be able to make more friends; and, finally, I will get to experience a semi-normal year of college. Though it was tough, I feel thankful for the support I received which gave me the strength to go back to school with my head held high and a stronger will to continue and complete my college education.

Pandemic 101: Teachable Lessons for All

By Monique N. Tookes

Many, like myself, feel like the pandemic is a real-life horror film. As a film enthusiast, I would compare the pandemic to the works of Alfred Hitchcock because of the way the ominous feeling of the virus crept into the woven fibers of our nation's consciousness. Any good horror film uses fear as a weapon of choice to drive the audience into a frenzy of emotions. I watched the news, in disbelief, as countless lives were consumed in China and India. Overnight, it seemed, what I was watching in foreign lands became a reality in the United States. As we all were winding down from a much-needed Spring Break from the routine of school, the hustle and bustle of work, and meetings on top of meetings, the entire world seemed to shut down under the weight of what would be called the COVID-19 pandemic.

The immediate impact hit over one weekend in Jacksonville, Florida. The entire Duval County Public School (DCPS) community learned that Spring Break would be extended due to the rise in COVID-19 cases. That extension would give way to a complete shutdown of physical school buildings. Not just the schools, but the entire non-educational community at large, except for what was considered essential; hospitals, grocery stores, gas stations, police, and fire departments. All activities came to a halt. We were sent home to focus on the family in a way we hadn't in years! Many had to learn their spouses and children all over again. No greater example of this reconnection was parents coming face to face with the realization that they really are and should be the chief educators in their children's lives. I must admit our children did have help as our educational system supplied an interactive learning platform called Duval Homeroom.

Many had to work from home and provide a learning environment for their children at the same time. Witnessing my son's senior year come to a screeching halt halfway through was sad. No prom, no senior activities, no spring sports (which meant he would not run track his last year of school), and graduation was put in peril. The shutdown produced major academic trauma. Parents had to decide if they needed to hold their children back due to the stress from the swift disconnect from their traditional academic systems. For my family, we had three in elementary school, one in middle school, and three in high school. We are grateful that we were able to close out successfully, and our senior was able to walk across the stage to receive his well-earned high school diploma.

> I would compare the pandemic to the works of Alfred Hitchcock because of the way the ominous feeling of the virus crept into the woven fibers of our nation's consciousness.

The 2020-2021 school year began with a hybrid model; some children returned to school campuses, and others continued with virtual platforms. We did the latter with our children. For our kindergartner and third-grader, it became painfully clear that the virtual platform was not working as both children needed additional resources that could only be successfully accommodated in a physical classroom. Trying to keep a five-year-old engaged on a computer for six hours was extreme torture. I would rather have my wisdom teeth pulled out without the numbing agent than endure that again! Our third-grader, who struggles in reading, simply was not connected and the technology was the culprit. Also, ten people all using in-home Wi-Fi proved to be problematic; there were days the activity shut our system down.

A heated debate arose among many parents about the importance of safety over education. Many felt, with the numbers still on the rise schools needed to remain closed, while others felt children were not thriving with online learning. An added side effect for some parents was waning productivity on the job while balancing watching children in a dual virtual environment. Being parents that did both, the decision was easy for us, all seven of our children went back to school. I was so grateful for a smooth transition back to in-person instruction because another issue was swirling around like a perfect storm. Our third grader always struggled with reading comprehension and writing. We discovered, after testing, that she showed signs of dyslexia. We were able to place her in a special academy to facilitate her unique way of learning.

> Our third grader always struggled with reading comprehension and writing. We discovered, after testing, that she showed signs of dyslexia.

The pandemic provided a bevy of opportunities for innovation with online tools to help in the classroom as well as state funding to our schools to provide summer bridge programs to remediate and refresh our children academically, for free. We were so excited that these summer school camps were there to ensure our children would be equipped to overcome the plight of the pandemic. Our kindergartner and rising fourth-grader attended the same camp and they loved it. They created new friends that overshadowed the fact they were going to school instead of enjoying the summer off. The great need to socialize after forced quarantine made the playground the place to be. We never had to wake them up or beg them to go, they were delighted to get themselves together and face each day with great expectations. As a parent, I even got an opportunity to grow as well!

It was the last day of summer school camp and the anticipation of our children coming home to replay how their day and the entire summer experience went was fragrant throughout our home like a Bath & Body Works plug-in. I was folding clothes in our room when our daughter burst through the door with the energy of most nine-year-olds, talking a mile a minute to her daddy who was in the corner of the room in his bequeathed office chair he got from his dad. She began to paint this seemingly bright tapestry of the last day of camp. She vividly expressed details about the friends she made, the remedial academic work they had to complete, and the field trips.

As overwhelmed as I was by a grateful heart, I was suddenly blindsided emotionally as I heard our daughter say, "I was reading in front of my class and the teacher said, "If I was going to the fourth grade, I should be able to read better than that." If you have ever been in an accident where the other car seemed to come from nowhere, you know how disoriented you can be. Once your brain makes the connection to what has happened, your whole body begins to jump into action. So, it was with me, after hearing our daughter share her classroom trauma, I snapped into MOMMY THE ADVOCATOR mode! I have always been a fierce defender of the underdog. From protecting kids on the playground, standing up to school leaders who were disenfranchising some of my peers, to defending my mother's parenting skills to my grandmother, I have known that I am hardwired to advocate on behalf of others.

When I asked my daughter the teacher's name, with great hesitation she responded. Our children already know me and so it's just easier to acquiesce to my request or suffer the consequences. I immediately called the school and asked to speak to the teacher in question. After having to call back three times, on the third call, the assistant principal answered and got me in contact with "Mr. Teacher."

"Hello Mr. Teacher, my name is Mrs. Tookes, and our daughter shared a very disturbing interaction she had with you. Can you walk me through what happened after our child publicly read material on the board and your response to her reading?" There was a short awkward pause; then Mr. Teacher responded like a bulldozer clearing the way for construction work to begin. "Your daughter was being silly reading very loud, and I told her as a fourth-grader she needed to read better than that. I don't play foolishness in my class!"

It is paramount to positively challenge people to bring about the change you want to see.

After our twelve-minute conversation concluded, a great teachable moment arrived that reminded us that our interpersonal skills were damaged during the 17 months since the pandemic began. The pandemic isolation created a lot of traumas, especially in how we communicate with each other. I learned I don't have to be infected by the fallout of the pandemic. It is paramount to positively challenge people to bring about the change you want to see. The realization that our daughter was overcoming an obstacle like dyslexia to read out loud became a celebration instead of a behavior problem. People, situations, and circumstances will offend you. Yet, how you respond and your motive for true resolve will determine how you handle yourself. I sow the type of seeds I want to harvest. My golden key here is to sow those seeds trusting that God will bring the harvest for everyone!

Patience During the Pandemic

By Melissa I. Walton Jones

"Patience is a virtue." The origin of that proverb is hard to find but it is straightforward in its meaning. Patience, as defined by Merriam Webster's online dictionary, is "the ability to wait for a long time without becoming annoyed or upset and the ability to remain calm and not become annoyed when dealing with problems or with difficult people." Once COVID-19 reared its ugly head, patience be damned.

Patience is, however, what I found during the pandemic in more ways than I could have ever imagined. It's important to note that being patient has its benefits. This journey with patience began March 13, 2020; it was the first day of Spring Break for my daughter and it was her last day of in-person school for the 2019-2020 school year. This would also be my unexpected and reluctant return to the fifth-grade classroom; having served as a substitute teacher to earn extra income for that grade level, while I was in college. The pandemic is also a teacher, and we all are in the same classroom. Some students listen and learn, while others misbehave or fall asleep. My misbehavior with my daughter was a pivotal moment, the first of many to come.

Like a lot of working parents, I had to juggle working full time from home while managing my child's remote learning experiences, managing my home and relationships, and other expectations and responsibilities. I left corporate America at the start of the pandemic and joined a non-profit organization as a finance leader. I onboarded and completed the first year with the company remotely. In doing so, I was able to actively assist in my daughter's remote learning experience, but the world as we knew it had come to a screeching halt, which challenged me immensely. It was and still is so very fascinating to think that we had been working at lightning speed and traveling the world and suddenly we had no choice but to pause and stop the over-activity. This is counterintuitive to the way I, and most of the world, operate. My personality is driven, typically through multitasking and operating at a high level of activity, across every area of my life. I tend to add additional things to my plate even though it may be quite full. I mean, I truly had enough going on and I was unknowingly adding more pressure and stress. I thought I could handle it, but the pandemic was such a dramatic shift for me. It's not like I didn't know patience before the pandemic, but I didn't understand that my level of patience was immature. Patience was exactly what I needed for the pandemic more than anything.

> The pandemic was a whirlwind with things changing every day and quickly. Businesses, services, and lives were shut down and people slowed down across the country and around the world.

The pandemic was a whirlwind with things changing every day and quickly. Businesses, services, and lives were shut down and people slowed down across the country and around the world. The state I live in was one of the first to issue stay-at-home orders; and as a result, I was sheltered in place with my family every day for more than a year. We enjoyed being able to spend so much more time together, and we took advantage of that. We had game nights, karaoke, mid-week movie nights, real reading time, pen pals, and study time for me. All my meetings became virtual gatherings, I didn't have to dress from the waist down, if I didn't want to, and I didn't have to spend time driving anywhere. So, there was definitely a benefit in saving time This was great, but before I could truly pivot and take advantage of things slowing down, things began to speed up again. It was as if a light bulb was switched on and we suddenly realized we had extra time. Consequently, it was assumed that this extra time should be filled with more virtual meetings, more conference calls, virtual happy hours – which were fun, but in general just more. I even made this assumption about myself and my personal level of activity. Suddenly I had more time, or so I thought. I filled my extra time with extra things. I found ways to keep myself busy, and even took on the added challenge of becoming a Certified Public Accountant. Strangely, I liked the downtime initially because I appreciated the added time I had to spend with my family, so in the beginning, I took full advantage of being quarantined. However, I kept wondering when things would go back to normal. The answer was extremely unclear then and even more so as I write this. I really don't think things will ever be normal again, and deep down I wasn't sure I wanted things to go back to what they were. For me, this caused undue levels of frustration and helplessness. I felt out of sorts and out of control at times. I imagine like many others, I managed it all the best I could for as long as I could, but I eventually found myself a little short with everyone and everything, especially patience. I realized to make life easier and more manageable I needed to strive for more patience with myself and others.

My lack of patience began to impact me not only physically, but emotionally in my connections with others and mentally in my tolerance of self. I couldn't even maintain my cool at times with my then 10-year-old daughter. It was in a specific exchange with her, in which she asked me a simple question that I realized patience was absent. When I raised my voice in response to her question, I opened my eyes to a problem. We mature and develop more patience when we intentionally slow down and become more mindful of our reactions and actions to ourselves and others. It helps to understand what triggers us and then consider our response rather than just react to situations. Being responsive means being intentional about our actions in word and deed. It requires a high level of self-awareness and emotional intelligence; it means taking a deep breath and not feeling threatened by any situation, no matter how daunting or challenging it may seem. As challenging as it is to build patience, the pandemic was the perfect time to sharpen the virtue.

Through practicing patience, you can increase your acceptance of what's happening in the present moment. On a practical level, that means transforming things such as traffic jams and helping with homework from frustration triggers to simple inconveniences that you understand and accept are out of your control.

Patience requires us to stop, breathe, observe, sense, and move slowly. Patience is and will continue to be essential for mental, physical, and spiritual survival during the pandemic and beyond. In slowing down and growing in patience, I could recall the words I'd heard so many times before, "patience is a virtue", but I also began to recall scriptures that have been such a driving part of my spiritual life. Patience is one of those eternal virtues that the scriptures simply will not stop going on about. *"Be patient in tribulation,"* it says in Romans 12:12. Ephesians 4:2 reads: *"Be completely humble and gentle; be patient, bearing with one another in love."* And one of my favorites, First Corinthians 13 sets the foundation of what true love is, beginning with three words, *"Love is patient…"* I learned that it's extremely critical to apply these things to myself, too. Through practicing patience, I learned to give myself grace.

We've come a long way since the beginning of the pandemic. We still have quite a way to go and practicing patience will help to get us there, even though it can be hard to do. It was hard for me, but I know that it can help us learn to enjoy the downtime and the in-between times, the traffic and grocery store lines, waiting on the elevator, and even helping a child through Common Core Math. The impatient me was anxious to fill the time between where I was and where I was going. The increasingly patient me instead engages my senses, appreciating life in the passing moments. Through practicing patience, you can increase your acceptance of what's happening in the present moment. On a practical level, that means transforming things such as traffic jams and helping with homework from frustration triggers to simple inconveniences that you understand and accept are out of your control. Through it all, I have made it and we will make it with a great dose of perseverance and patience. The ongoing pandemic is proof positive that patience is a valuable and vital virtue, truly.

And Still I Rise

Commit or Quit

By Kristin Harper

> *"For I know the plans I have for you,"*
> *declares the LORD, "plans to prosper you*
> *and not to harm you, plans to give you hope*
> *and a future."* (Jeremiah 29:11, KJV)

A friend posted a couple of thought-provoking questions on Facebook: "When did you know it was time to step out on faith and explore new professional opportunities? What was that moment in your life when you felt a nudge to make a change?" Among the dozens of answers, there were several recurring themes:

- You've mastered the role and accomplished your goals.

- You're no longer learning and have become complacent.

- You feel unappreciated.

- Your joy is gone, and work feels more like a burden.

- You dread going to work and even cry. (I was amazed how many people mentioned crying).

- Your mental and physical health is compromised.

- Your role is eliminated, or your services are no longer needed.
- There's a gap between your value and your pay.
- You have greater ambitions, goals, and purpose than the job can fulfill.

Whatever the feeling or reason, when the questions linger in your spirit like a nagging child tugging at your clothing begging for a piece of candy, it's a clear signal that they deserve consideration.

I've personally experienced many of these sentiments and situations. After a massive acquisition at the company I worked at in 2019, the organizational dynamics were changing, and I felt restless. While I was a strong performer and leader within the company, the work no longer brought me joy. I'd spent the better part of my career leading global iconic brands, innovation, and marketing. However, those skills didn't align with what the job required or what the company needed. I was at a crossroads.

In our lives, moments of stillness bring clarity, and it became clear just how much I'd sacrificed, how hard I'd worked, and how exhausted I felt.

It weighed on my spirit for months, not as agony, but as quiet contemplation and persistent prayer. Nothing and no one pushed me away. I could have easily stayed in my role, but I know myself. A slow-growing, unspoken disdain would have spread like a cancerous cell to my colleagues and family. I was hungry for more, but not so impatient that I made any sudden moves. I waited for months to hear from God, and when I did, I made a decision.

Commit or quit, just don't quit, and stay.

Like people, jobs come into your life for a reason, a season, or a lifetime. When you're at a crossroads, one of the worst things you can do is straddle the fence. After much prayer, deliberation, and heart-to-heart talks with my husband, we prepared financially (upon his suggestion), set an exit date, and I made the leap from being a Global Vice President of a Fortune 20 company to becoming a full-time entrepreneur. I defied conventional wisdom. I didn't have a written business plan. I had no clients in the cue. What I had, though, was an unshakable faith and a God who has ordered every step from then to now. And if the truth be told, before I was even formed in my mother's womb, God had a plan for my life that I'm striving every day to fulfill. He has a plan for your life, too.

After nearly 20 years of working in Corporate America, I gave myself a week to decompress. In our lives, moments of stillness bring clarity, and it became clear just how much I'd sacrificed, how hard I'd worked, and how exhausted I felt. That second week, though, I put pen to paper to develop a plan of action. It was November 2019, and my plan was to promote my book which was published in the summer of 2020 – *The Heart of a Leader: 52 Emotional Intelligence Insights to Advance Your Career.* The book provided a platform to give keynotes and lead training for corporations and conferences. However, I quickly learned that the words 2020 and plans didn't go together in the same sentence.

The pandemic interrupted any plans I thought I had, which forced me to go back to the drawing board. I'd walked away from a six-figure salary and lucrative compensation package, and there's no way I was going to let my family down, or my new business fail. After enrolling in the online Goldman Sachs 10,000 Women Initiative for Entrepreneurs, I went through a simple, yet methodical process to identify a core target audience, their unmet needs, my capabilities, and differentiators – the steps I'd taken many times leading product innovation, but now for my own business.

Given my professional experiences leading brands like Crest®, Oral-B®, and Hershey's KISSES®, it was natural to target corporations with branded products and services. For as far back as I can remember, I've had two areas of passion: 1) growing businesses and brands, and 2) developing people, which is what inspired me to write the book. In May 2020, a call with a former market research vendor turned to friend and mentor, changed everything, and God's plan for my business became clear.

Semi-retired at the time, Kaylie Dugan was CEO of Imaginologie for 20 years, a market research firm that specialized in ethnography research and had dozens of Fortune 500 and agency clients. In fact, we met in 2007 when I was a young Brand Manager. I loved her approach to market research so much that I hired her at every other company I worked for.

If you believe in divine providence, you know that nothing is by accident. Every situation and experience has prepared you for this moment.

During our call, Kaylie shared, "I've never said this to anyone, but you could do what I did," and the rest is history. She is now VP of Imaginologie, a division of Driven to Succeed, and together with our agile, dynamic team, we combine head and heart to **Bring Insights to Life**™ through mentally and visually engaging, multi-media reports. I've gone from a solopreneur to a team of 16 people in less than a year, and during a global pandemic at that. It's only by the grace of God.

At Driven to Succeed, we lead market research, brand strategy, and brainstorming to help brands innovate and grow. Our point of differentiation is delivering insightful market research in a fun, memorable way that our competition can't or won't do. It's Kaylie's superpower – creating colorful, visually engaging graphic reports that fly in the face of long, bullet-point-laden PowerPoint decks. Having been her client several times, I am ecstatic to not only carry on Kaylie's legacy but to take it to the next level by combining my skills in marketing, branding, and P&L (profit and loss) management.

> *"And the LORD answered me, and said, Write the vision, and make it plain upon tables, that he may run that readeth it."* (Habakkuk 2:2, KJV)

Several years ago, I took time to write down specific goals and visions that I had for my life. As a classically trained brand marketer, I'd become skilled at completing OGSMs for business – that is, Objectives, Goals, Strategies, and Measures. So, I applied that same discipline to my life. I'm always filled with wonder when visions become reality, whether written or in the form of a vision board collage.

In 2016, my objective read as follows: "To leverage my God-given talents and life experiences to transform insight into strategies and visions into reality." Isn't it interesting that the essence of market research is to discover insights, and that our niche is **Transforming Insights into 'So What' and 'Now What'™**? God has blessed my business abundantly. While my team actively engages in business development activities, 90% of our clients have come through word of mouth, and we already have repeat Fortune 500 clients. I truly give God the glory.

> *"And we know that all things work together for good to them that love God, to them who are the called according to his purpose."* (Romans 8:28, KJV)

If you believe in divine providence, you know that nothing is by accident. Every situation and experience has prepared you for this moment. They are building blocks that give you strength, know-how, and clarity.

Whether you're at a crossroads, or simply committed to fulfilling your God-given purpose, I challenge you to think about your life, including but not limited to your job or profession, and take time to reflect on the following OGSM questions:

- What is the highest vision you have of your life?
- What is your long-term objective?
- What are your short-term goals?
- Who are you serving? Who is your flock?
- What value do you add to people and organizations?
- What strategies and tactics can/will you implement to realize your vision, objective, and goals?
- What are calculated risks you can take to learn and grow?
- How will you measure success for each strategy and tactic?
- Who will you engage to support you on this journey?

If the pandemic has taught us anything, it's reinforced that life is dynamic and change can be swift. So, I encourage you to put pen to paper to articulate your unique purpose, callings, and gifts; clarify your vision; then move with intention to realize the highest version of yourself in a way that brings God glory.

My Pre-Pandemic Pivot

By Jeri A. Dyson, M.D.

My personal pivot began five years before the global pivot known as the COVID-19 pandemic. I was working in my dream career as a physician at The President's Hospital, Bethesda Naval Medical, (renamed Walter Reed Military Medical Center at Bethesda). From the outside, I was living the life. I had an extremely impressive curriculum vitae and was the doctor to the children of the world's most powerful and influential people. My expertise in young adult medicine and sexually transmitted infections and my reputation for delivering complicated medical information in an understandable comedic style opened doors to work within the entertainment industry. I was traveling incessantly, domestically, and abroad, educating teens, and anyone else who would listen, about HIV/AIDS. I was a well-paid single physician making extra money as a landlord. My family was healthy. I had a robust bank account, my car was paid in full, and I had the ability to buy whatever I desired. My life was fantastic, that is, until I started burning the candle at both ends.

Before you start rolling your eyes and thinking, "this lady is full of herself," stay with me. I'm sharing my life before my personal pandemic, the same one that prepared me for this global pandemic. With all the work and traveling, I noticed I was often fatigued and drained. Regardless of how much recovery sleep I got, I never felt rested. My primary physician, a holistic medicine doctor, warned me I would burn myself into an adrenal crisis if I continued with the accept-all-challenges-and-push-through-it-sis stance. She suggested I take a six-month sabbatical to rest. It sounded like the fastest way to commit career suicide, so I ignored her. Eighteen months after that visit; all hell broke loose.

It started with me requiring surgery for hemorrhaging fibroids. After the surgery, my recovery was slow. Carrying the heaviest patient load at the time, I was drained and overworked. Despite asking for a schedule change with the possibility of working part-time, my requests were denied. I knew resigning from my high-status job was my only choice, especially after refusing to sign a revised mandatory off-duty employment agreement. The mandate to sign this new document was issued while I was on a trip to Ghana. The document I had signed just three months prior had gone from one and a half pages to eight pages. (Yes, I counted them.)

I knew what I had to do. It was time to pivot. I resigned. Lesson 1: Do not sacrifice your livelihood for your loyalty.

What stood out to me was that I was the only person in my division required to sign it. The other physicians fell under different contractual agreements, so they did not need to sign them. I knew what I had to do. It was time to pivot. I resigned.

Lesson 1: Do not sacrifice your livelihood for your loyalty. We are often loyal to jobs at the expense of our livelihood. Your job should add value to your life, not just money to your bank account. Anything - job, relationship, or external commitment that withdraws more than it supplies will eventually leave you depleted.

Two years after my resignation, the other previous positions that competed for my attention were nowhere to be found. Like how others pursue you while you're in a committed relationship, yet somehow you become less attractive to them the more available you are.

In a nutshell, over the five-year period, I tried all types of flexible physician gigs. I was traveling all over the states seeing patients in their homes, but I was still exhausted. I lost my financial status, my home, and some fair-weathered friends along for the ride. I ended up filing bankruptcy, and just when I thought I was getting back on my feet, my back broke - literally. I sustained two spontaneous vertebral compression fractures and broken ribs. A week later, we discovered the fractures resulted from a blood cancer that affected my bone marrow, causing me to produce abnormal plasma cells. Plasma cells are responsible for creating antibodies, and antibodies are the cells that help fight infections. That explanation is super-simplified, but I'm certain you understand. Those things I was concerned about previously became irrelevant. My life was all that mattered. With that diagnosis, I realized again; it was time to pivot.

Lesson 2: Forgive quickly, heal your soul, and the body will follow. Let that sh*t go and live! Needless to say, during chemotherapy and my bone marrow transplant, I became avoidant of any and everyone who could make me ill, which was everyone. The transplant left me totally immunocompromised. Because I had no immune defense any minor infection would have landed me in critical care. My life was just like the 1976 movie *The Boy in the Plastic Bubble* starring John Travolta. So many adjustments had to be made to remain healthy and allow my body to heal. To give you an example of the extreme measures we had to adopt, I could not receive or be around fresh flowers because the microbes and bacteria found on flowers were liable to make me deathly ill. I felt so isolated from everything and everyone. Those moments of insulation became instrumental to my overall healing. I had time to go deep within myself to decide how I wanted life to be.

How could my life transition from abundance to brokenness in every form and every definition of the word? Where did I make the wrong turn? That five-year period was one of the absolute worst parts of my life, but it was also one of the best parts because I found my true self during that transformative time. I knew there must be a bigger purpose on this life path, even with its twists and turns. Instead of feeling sorry for myself, I decided to change my perspective during that very dark period. I had to reorient my soul to better heal my body. Every place that the soles of my feet touched, I carved out a path for my soul's healing. During my healing, I learned to restructure everything from my eating habits to napping and self-care. I became grateful for my ability to do little things like walking unassisted, taking deep breaths without cracking a rib, receiving hugs, or even lying flat. These are just a few things I was unable to do early on in my cancer treatment. As time went on, I was able to stand from a seated position without using a walker. The more gratitude I expressed, the faster I healed. I also reassigned more significance to things that really mattered, like family, health, rest, and true friendships. The isolation was working in my favor. My new patterns of thought began to show in my external life. I was able to secure a national SAG-AFTRA commercial for women surviving all types of cancers. The weight loss and vegan lifestyle had me looking younger and more vibrant. I began modeling in print and traveling to share my story. My creativity was at an all-time high.

My depth of gratitude was expanded even further during the 2020 global pandemic. When the global pandemic hit, I continued to do what I had been doing for the previous two years. I used my lockdown to journal, photograph scenery, which was now void of people, and write creatively. From my writings and photography, I created healing cards called "Sole to Soul Journey ~ Heal Thyself." I knew others were feeling the brunt of the physical and emotional isolation caused by the global lockdown. So, I created what I used during my isolation to help people center themselves and get through it. With so many deaths surrounding us and the movement restrictions placed on people, I wanted people to take advantage of the downtime to really rest, connect with loved ones (however possible), and heal. Heal their relationships, heal their finances, heal their limiting beliefs, heal their homes. It was healing time, but I also realized that people needed to heal in their own way and at their own pace. I believe once the soul begins its healing process, all good things are pulled toward that soul. "Sole to Soul Journey" has since evolved to include serenity bath soaks, candles, and other things we need for self-care and healing.

> That five-year period was one of the absolute worst parts of my life, but it was also one of the best parts because I found my true self during that transformative time.

Lesson 3: It is not your responsibility to heal others. It is your responsibility to discover those things within that cause dis-ease and heal them. That is your only goal. Go be healed.

Pivotal Plays

By Anjylla Y. Foster, Ph.D.

I was not in a position mentally, physically, or emotionally to conquer spring 2020. I was suffering from a personal problem where ambition, financial motivators, and eagerness to be productive causes you to move at a pace impossible to sustain without regard for the impact to your well-being. I was just running. I wasn't making strategic moves. I was running sprints until my internal whistle blew telling me to stop. In March 2020, on a Thursday, my team canceled badminton practice due to a possible COVID case. I stayed home from my full-time job due to the uncertainty of exposure. The next day, I went to work to gather the belongings I would need for a two-week closure.

On that Sunday, I was asked to help prepare to close my part-time job for a two-week closure. After a month of closure, I was furloughed from my position as a Server Trainer. The state of Illinois canceled high-school sports for the remainder of the season. In-person classes were canceled. I had to find creative ways to do my full-time job virtually until we reopened. I also had to stop working on a dissertation. I needed to learn how to better use my time on the court. I could not keep sprinting. I needed to pause.

Learn an innovative strategy play. Learn how to make moves to the basket. Learn to pivot.

Once upon a time, I was playing basketball seven days a week. If I played today, you would think I was the team manager and not an accidental three-year varsity player. We would run drill after drill after drill in hopes of applying a skill to practical play. One of my love-hate drills involved a player posting up against the defense and working on pivot moves toward the hoop. I was short for my position as a power forward so I needed all the creativity that a coach could cultivate. I would often have to guard my best friend because she was most comparable in height to the opponents I'd guard, but she had a competitive edge: elbows. My Lord, that girl had pivots with elbows to your chest or face for days. She was the queen of the "up and under" which consisted of a fake toward the hoop and a half step in a semi-lateral direction, also toward the hoop. She mastered and excelled at that quick move because of how she positioned her elbows. Those elbows could ward off an army. She protected that ball to score like it was the last thing on Earth she might do.

> The pandemic forced me to practice pivots and now I'm in the game. I don't even think it's half-time yet, but I'm not aimlessly sprinting on the court anymore.

She's still my best friend. She was the main source of sanity in my quarantine pod. The story isn't about her though (although she has been a constant cheerleader through my own pivots). The story is about practicing how to pivot, although the skill of pivoting never quite translates until you're in the game. The pandemic forced me to practice pivots and now I'm in the game. I don't even think it's half-time yet, but I'm not aimlessly sprinting on the court anymore. I learned to use my elbows to be more effective when I'm making moves. The story is about how sometimes, you can pivot all you want, run as fast as you can, and still end up in the same place. As the world began to re-open, I was slowly finding myself in the same place. I was sprinting nowhere, fast. I had to remind myself how to pivot with a purpose.

Here is what I told myself:

1. Practice your pivot. Most of us did not get a chance to prepare for metaphorical pivots of the pandemic. We were forced into our pivots by a mismanaged global health pandemic. Now that you know what it's like to be isolated from the world, keep practicing your pivot. Practice the moment the pandemic turned in a positive direction for you even if that was a brief period. The time you spend away from friends and family, continue to do it. The time away from work, how can you recreate that without hindering your financial stability? Maybe you shouldn't practice for months at a time but find an amount of time that allows you to remember what it's like to be alone. If your pivot consists of trying new or different things, don't stop. Continue to experience the sensation of having time to try and discover something new: making bread pudding from nearly stale bagels, enjoying a faux-competitive match-up of hip-hop icons, or crafting door decor from faux flowers you've found in your home during a Zoom happy hour.

2. Use your elbows. Listen, if you're not protecting your peace, joy, heart, head, health, and priorities, re-evaluate your pivot. We'll talk more about that later, but the skill requires you to use your elbows. You get to decide how much physical or social distancing remains between you and others. You are in control! You don't have to engage with humans who drain your energy. Stick those elbows out and acknowledge them from a distance. Don't go back to stimulating poor work relationships as a job security strategy. The elbow can be a dangerous weapon

when it makes contact with an ear, eye, or chest. No, don't go literally elbowing folks. Find the tact and diplomacy needed to show people who you are and whose you are. Pivot into the hearts and chests of people who need to feel your presence. Pivot toward the ears of those who silenced you into questioning the power of your own voice. Use those elbows wisely and as needed. I have become a firm believer in simple elbow bumps as a presence of my own power. I don't know you; you don't get a hug, but you can have this elbow. I'm no longer transferring the energy of my mind, heart, or soul without extensive vetting. Yet, you are more than welcome to feel the power that lies within these elbows.

3.   Pivoted back. Some pivoted back. The world opened again, and we went back to the same habits we had prior to the pandemic. We work four jobs to create the quality of life we're accustomed to. We say yes to most friend functions because we'd feel like a bad friend if we said no. We go to the job we don't really like because we're simply grateful to still have a job. It's okay. I hope you've found a place that will allow you to pivot. You can keep pivoting. I'd suggest staying out of the proverbial lane (you only have a few seconds in there in a basketball game). If you're in the lane and start to feel pressure, breathe. Use your elbows. Pass the ball to a teammate or take the shot. The funny thing about a pivot is, if you do it too much for too long, you're liable to end up where you started - especially in basketball. If you pick up that pivot foot, it's a penalty against you. So, while you pivot, you may find yourself back where you started, but there's always room for a creative distraction and lateral move to get you closer to the basket. If you're not ready for that, keep pivoting. Practice. Use your elbows. That's what I told myself.

The opportunity to write about my pivotal moment allowed me to take the time to assess what quarter I am in. My pivots are leading to new opportunities. I am setting new expectations for myself. I am setting new boundaries. I am finding moments that bring me joy. I am learning what energizes me. I am discovering what I need to sustain a level of excellence that I am proud of. When I find myself reverting to old sprinting habits, I stop. It's okay to stop. Fortunately, the pandemic has taught me to be more strategic when I sprint so that I don't have to stop, but maybe do a move that better gets me to where I think I want to go. I sprint with purpose now. I sprint with the purpose to execute a play. I sprint with expectations and boundaries that I choose to set for myself. I sprint with the whistle around my neck and a pivot in mind.

My pivots are leading to new opportunities. I am setting new expectations for myself. I am setting new boundaries. I am finding moments that bring me joy.

When I THINK of HOME…

By Jylla Moore Tearte, Ph.D.

Unannounced. Uninvited. Unexpected. Uncontrollable. With absolute disrespect for the protocol of announcing a visit to someone's home, the coronavirus pandemic dropped in. It didn't say how long we would have to shelter in place. It just invaded my space. It didn't say my home would become not only the place to sleep but also the place to eat cooked meals (because restaurants closed). The invasion meant home became my only office, as work-from-home was no longer a choice but a requirement. The prolonged invasion meant home became my online shopping mall and grocery store complete with delivery by brave souls who were still OUT. Visits to the beauty salon were ended and my hubby became my personal stylist. Home became our place of worship, and we were attending church from Florida in Atlanta, Cincinnati, and Virginia, virtually, every Sunday or watching the replay during the week. IT—that pandemic—even closed the beach down!

Home alone was real and I was a forced attendee in the production. Except, there was no makeup under the mask for this performer since lipstick merely rubbed off on the covering fabric.

The wardrobe change was redundant. The same wash and wear lounge set, sometimes with the bottoms, other times, without. I thought that a condo on the ocean, complete with beautiful sunrises, sunsets, and walks along the beach was my dream home. This was NOT the HOME of my dreams. This was not the home that Dorothy dreamed and sang about in *The Wiz*, a soulful rendition of the childhood classic movie *The Wizard of Oz*, or the home that actors and vocalists Billy Porter and MJ Rodriguez sang about in their rendition of "Home."

I had never had a pause in my life, even though I had often wondered what my introverted self would do if I had more time alone in my home. I didn't have any warning and this intruder, COVID-19, proceeded to build a bubble within the bubble with just me and my husband together for days. Then days became weeks and weeks became months. When would this imprisonment end? The dining room table became the command center at six A.M. for days on end as we intently managed five devices trying to win the vaccine lottery. I sank deeper and deeper into my thoughts: Would I finally get a shot at my shot? Would the vaccine work? Would I ever be able to escape my secluded lifestyle? It became harder and harder to GET OUT!

> I didn't have any warning and this intruder, COVID-19, proceeded to build a bubble within the bubble with just me and my husband together for days. Then days became weeks and weeks became months.

I thought about the home of my childhood as I binge watched the FX Network television show "Pose", the story of finding a home in New York City's underground ball culture during the height of the AIDS epidemic. My childhood home was blueberry pancakes as a treat; dinner at the kitchen table on Sunday afternoons with family and whoever showed up; and grilled cheese and bologna sandwiches on Sunday night right before our favorite television show, "Bonanza" came on in black and white. My pandemic home exposed my forgotten gratitude to appreciate that my rose-colored glasses did not reveal my blessing of a home that had not been that same experience or memory of home in everyone's life.

As I navigated behind the walls in my house, I relived conversations with Dr. Dorothy Height, founder of the National Council of Negro Women (NCNW) as she shared her dream of a home for African American Women between the White House and the U.S. Capitol building. After the NCNW Building became a reality, I would visit her office and as she talked, I would be in awe of the comfort in her space. My library of books brought no comfort.

As I slowly walked through the NCNW Room at the National Museum of African American History and Culture the night before it officially opened to the public in 2016, I realized that I was standing in the room alone until the Honorable Alexis Herman, Former Secretary of the United States Department of Labor, walked in. We exchanged pleasantries, but I felt that we had both gravitated to this space with Dr. Height as we looked at the large table in the center of the room. We were home in that space.

Memories of home that surfaced during the pandemic pause in my home were so visceral. Dr. Height's invitation to have tea in Poet and Author Dr. Maya Angelou's garden in Winston-Salem with just a small group of women resurfaced in my memory. As I walked through Dr. Angelou's home, I was transfixed on the shelves of books behind her desk as we approached the garden. The afternoon tea provided the opportunity to bond with phenomenal women who gathered and created lifelong memories. Every home I have lived in since that day, I have assured books were on shelves or tables throughout my home and that guests could pull up to the table for a conversation or just for a cup of tea. Books and guests did not comfort in the pandemic home.

During the pandemic, I was haunted daily with never-ending posts and news stories of deaths from COVID-19 and then the Delta Variant. I hoped that only fun and beautiful memories would be forever remembered in the homes of their loved ones. I am grateful that my mother-in-love escaped COVID's visit to her assisted living community. Daily pandemic updates of hot spots during the lockdown delivered not only a heart-wrenching reality but stirred cause for constant prayer. The mental gymnastics were exhausting.

I missed my friends. The pandemic separated us. We would often have special events to celebrate various occasions. I looked at pictures from the celebrations at restaurants with my sister girlfriends in Chicago, the HUES. We always experienced unabashed energy and unequaled joy in each other's presence. Christmas 2019 was the last such gathering. I loved gatherings and entertaining because people always found connections and common bonds that lifted spirits, inspired the journey ahead, and supplied downtime from the hectic pace of the world.

What I missed most was family. Family by blood and family by choice. It was anxiety inducing not to be able to jump on a plane or even drive 20 hours, if I needed, to get to my family. We missed special moments and events. I don't know that there could have been a greater joy in life than when our daughter completed the mandatory ten-day quarantine for out-of-state visitors to Florida at an area hotel when she visited for the Christmas 2020 holiday. We had been physically separated for eleven months, the longest span of time in her three decades of life. When you give birth to a child and have a special relationship with them, separation is difficult. With no regard for the separation of relationships, the pandemic also gave no consideration to the onset of concern and worry families would endure. We missed socializing. We missed our friends. We missed our grandsons. We missed our family.

Deciding to move was my pivotal moment.

Months before the world gradually re-opened, we had confidently solidified plans to relocate to a place where we could be present and ready for our next chapter in life with family and friends. The pandemic pause influenced the design elements, the heart elements, the location, and the circle for our future bubble home design.

I would suggest that wherever you are, right now, that you create your dream home. Whether you have moved or are planning to move, think of this pivot as competition for the greatest HOMEcoming on Earth. Envision the laughter, the special moments, and places in the space that will be home. Design the space for flowers from the garden or from your favorite local market. Think of your home as an oasis, as a wise and worldly woman shared with me on a bus one night at a conference in Arizona. Change the colors of the pillows. Tidy up and donate the excess. Hang a quote or inspirational picture on the wall. Even better - create your own inspired art. What does your space invite you to experience and to enjoy?

> The good news through it all, we found a beautiful natural flow of life in our bubble together and I know I experienced living in a HOME where love was overflowing.

The good news through it all, we found a beautiful natural flow of life in our bubble together and I know I experienced living in a HOME where love was overflowing. There were gifts during the silence that would have been drowned out by the noise of life. Did you discover a new kind of love in your bubble? Are you exploring how to increase love, tenfold, in your life? Is the space where you live your retreat? I am passionate about being prepared for uninvited guests moving forward and living in a home created by design.

The Journey Continues…

Pearls and Faith Over Fear

By Vesta Godwin Clark

My mother and grandmother live with my husband and I in our home in Newark, New Jersey. Nanny is 99 and feisty; and as a caregiver, my days are long, but my heart is overjoyed with the generations of love that I experience on a daily basis (often in the early morning hours).

I have served as the Executive Director for St. James Social Service Corporation (SJSSC) in Newark, New Jersey, since 1999. From a renovated historic mansion in the middle of the neighborhood, I lead an agency that operates a soup kitchen and one of the largest food pantries in Essex County. It has always been a daily challenge to provide food for individuals in the community we serve. Finding funding, resources, and partnerships to secure food and to pay a living wage to a staff of 11 people, consumes my days. Yet, I never lost sight that this work is my life's calling. Our team lives our mission that "helping people is not an option, it's a way of life!"

As we work diligently to fulfill our mission, it is difficult to help others understand that some people just did not have the capacity, for so many reasons, to have what many take for granted - FOOD. We are proud providers in our community who close each day in the office with prayer. We witness moments when those prayers are answered, other days we wonder if the prayers were heard. Yet, we were a well-oiled machine, running often on autopilot, serving the community, and lifting people out of their temporary situation to experience better days, even if it was as simple as a meal one evening or food for a week.

Having a cook was critical to our mission, so for the first time in January 2020, I stepped out on faith and hired a cook to handle the soup kitchen so that those needing a hot meal would have access. For a myriad of other tasks, we depend upon hundreds of volunteers who fulfill their passion for service by helping to organize the food pantry, serve food and distribute the donations. The audience we served looked mostly like me (African American) and were primarily from the local community, the Central Ward of Newark.

Our mission did not cease because of the Governor's decision. Our neighbors without homes still needed to eat and our clients who were regulars to our food pantry had no resources to purchase food from the grocery store.

Then, everything changed. CO-VID-19 reared its ugly, vicious head. The Governor of New Jersey announced that people had to stay in their homes. People could not go to work. Offices closed. Schools shut down. The doors of churches closed. Only grocery stores and pharmacies remained open as essential resources for people. Hospitals and the staffs became frontline for people who needed care. At great personal risk, they kept their vow to care for people. No vaccine. Scarce personal protection equipment.

St. James Social Service Corporation fell into the open hands of the stay-at-home dictate and our clientele found no safety net of protection from falling through the cracks. In some cases, they were homeless. In others, they struggled with paying the rent when jobs were eliminated or businesses closed down. They became caregivers to generations of family members, all under the same roof, with very little opportunity to practice social distancing.

The SJSSC staff was faced with the decision of staying home or risking our lives and that of our families to come and serve those who would need our services more than ever. Being exposed to COVID was a real fear. Our volunteers, the massive resources that supported the work, had to stay home, yet our mission did not cease because of the Governor's decision. Our neighbors without homes still needed to eat and our clients who were regulars to our food pantry had no resources to purchase food from the grocery store. People still needed to eat and SJSSC's calling was to provide food. But with the stay-at-home order in effect, I did not know what to do. As the often-defiant, make-a-way out of no way leader and believer, I called the New Jersey Lt. Governor, Sheila Oliver, who knew the story of SJSSC and I posed the question: "What are people who don't have the means to purchase food from the grocery store, even though it's open, supposed to do?" She responded the next day saying she had approved a grant for $150,000 so that we could continue to operate. That was a blessing for the people who were dependent upon our agency to provide food and to the staff that was two weeks behind in pay.

I convened a meeting with the team of 11 which included my administrative staff. Would they be willing to stay open and continue to fulfill our mission? After many questions and careful consideration, we decided as a team to stay open. The only exception was our cook. She had four school-aged children and their risks were exacerbated with the dynamics of their virtual schooling needs. I understood her concern. I went home each evening to two women I love dearly who were considered high risk. Staying open increased our empathy for those in our homes. After two weeks of angst, she decided to return to the team as a result of an offer to bring her children to work while she cooked. During her two weeks of absence, a client who was homeless and who frequented our soup kitchen volunteered to cook!

When jobs were lost and cupboards became bare, people came from New York, Pennsylvania, and other counties and cities in New Jersey to receive groceries from our emergency food pantry and to-go meals from the soup kitchen. Professionals who were forced to leave Wall Street and high-rise offices found themselves in lines that wrapped around the corner for food at SJSSC. Our lines increased when unemployment benefits were delayed, when people who had been living paycheck to paycheck lost their jobs, when children had to stay home and miss school meals, and parents had to set up a home office when they were forced to work, if they had work, virtually. Everything changed.

For the first two and a half months of the pandemic, SJSSC was the only food pantry within a 100-mile radius that never closed during the stay-at-home order. Our community of need became much larger. The people in need became greater and COVID-19 did not discriminate by color or income level. The lines for both the soup kitchen and the food pantry were longer than ever and kept growing every day. We served no less than 500 people daily. Seeing entire families drive up to receive lunch or dinner in to-go plates was heartbreaking. The demographics and the clientele shifted dramatically as the pandemic stretched into an undetermined, unknown, and unpredictable state of potential re-opening.

Our light became the four children who joined their mother at work every day. Their innocence by not having had a defined reality, routine or firm set of expectations prior to the pandemic provided a vision that reminded us of our mission as we watched them navigate their school work; their engagement with packing bags of potatoes; turning the dining room into a study hall or a sea of toys to keep the little ones busy as the older children completed homework assignments. The staff had a frontline example, daily, of being able to touch the life of a child. We remained encouraged that we could touch the lives of our clients in a similar way as we looked for the pearls in the moments that kept us lifted. It was with that imagery that the four girls received pearls from Auntie Vesta on inauguration day for Vice President Kamala Harris. They were encouraged to see themselves as anyone they aspired to become, including "Boss Lady Miss Vesta."

When the world shut down, my staff and I left the safety of our homes, came to work, and prayed together daily. We were blessed to have our SJSSC work pod. For 18 months, the staff was exposed to thousands of clients. Our greatest fear was having to close because of COVID. When testing became available, the entire team went for the first time together. After months of staying COVID-free, one staff member tested positive, for the anti-bodies. During the height of the pandemic, she had taken a couple of days off with allergy-like symptoms not realizing she had been exposed at some point. That was as close as the staff came to contracting COVID. I am grateful that my entire staff remained COVID-free and thankful that our families and friends were protected and safely navigated this call-to-action with us.

> When the world shut down, my staff and I left the safety of our homes, came to work, and prayed together daily. We were blessed to have our SJSSC work pod.

We are encouraged by stories from our clients. I think about an attorney, who prior to the pandemic, was an immigration lawyer in New York City. When her job was eliminated, she found herself needing food and falling behind on rent. She became dependent upon SJSSC as she struggled to stay above water. Eventually, she was able to find a new opportunity as a lawyer helping people being evicted. Her story is just one of many. These stories never end. Our work never ends.

This snapshot in time only provides cause for pause. The food pantry and soup kitchen remain open. We know that this pandemic is not over. It raises its ugly head in the forms of chaos and consistently changing struggles. The struggle increased ten-fold during the COVID-19 crisis. It is still on the rise. The implications of providing food, helping with housing, and filling basic needs continue for people who pass through the doors of SJSSC; and the staff continues to leave the doors open. We are ever watchful for a glimmer of light to share with the world. It is why we unabashedly fight to serve our clients. SJSSC is a passion that requires faith over fear as we continue to look for pearls of wisdom and for servant hearts who are called to give back, to never forget or be judgmental of someone else's journey.

> This snapshot in time only provides cause for pause. The food pantry and soup kitchen remain open. We know that this pandemic is not over. It raises its ugly head in the forms of chaos and consistently changing struggles.

"For there is always light, if only we're brave enough to see it."

– Amanda Gorman

Author Profiles

Rev. Teraleen R. Campbell

An award-winning author, speaker and certified coach, Evangelist Teraleen R. Campbell serves several organizations within her community in the Washington, DC suburban area. One who knows the worth of prayer, she loves to intercede on behalf of the needs of God's people and serves as lead intercessor each month for a local non-profit organization.

A survivor of childhood domestic abuse, at the hands of her stepfather, Teraleen is a tireless advocate against domestic violence. She participates in events which address this issue. Her community involvement has garnered recognition from professional, faith-based, and non-profit organizations such as the March of Dimes, Be the Match, and Taylor Thomas of WHUR Radio.

Her ministry extends to Zeta Phi Beta Sorority, Inc. She authored the sorority's Centennial Prayer and facilitated the Global Day of Prayer for several years. She also was a co-author for *Faith of Our Founders*, which is the sorority's devotional book.

No stranger to providing encouragement through the written word, Teraleen has co-authored five books. Additionally, she released to the award-winning *From Carefree to Caregiver* in 2018. She created Caregivers Connect online support group and has become known as the Caregiver to caregivers. Through this online community she provides caregivers with resources, support, and valuable information. Her newest release *Embracing Your New Normal Devotional* provides support after the loss of a loved one.

Website: Teraleencampbell.com
Facebook, Twitter & Instagram: Teraleen Campbell

Vesta Godwin Clark

Vesta Godwin Clark has been the Executive Director of *St. James Social Service Corporation (SJSSC)* located in Newark since 1999. The agency is one of the largest providers of food in Essex County. The COVID19 pandemic forced Vesta and her staff to become "Essential" employees. As the only provider of emergency food open during the first 2 months of the pandemic, distributing outside, without volunteers, food was given to more than 32,000 people! In April 2020, the agency was featured on the Foodnetwork's *Restaurant Impossible* entitled *Quarantine Check-in* with Chef Robert Irvine as a follow-up to their 2010 makeover segment. The agency was also highlighted on ABC's Nightline during the pandemic.

A graduate of Rutgers University, Vesta holds a Master of Arts degree in Public Administration from William Paterson University and a Certificate in Public and Non-Profit Management.

She joined Zeta Phi Beta Sorority, Inc. in 1980 and is a charter member of Gamma Kappa Chapter. A Life Member, Vesta has held positions on all levels in the sorority which includes National Second Vice President and New Jersey State Director. She is an active member of Eta Omicron Zeta Chapter.

Active in her community, Vesta was appointed by Newark Mayor Ras Baraka to the Workforce Development Board where she is Vice Chairman. She also served two terms on the Rutgers University Board of Trustees where she was the youngest elected Alumnae Trustee.

A member of Saint James AME Church, Newark, Vesta is married to Sigma Brother, Rev. Reginald V. Clark. Through marriage and Zeta; she has four children and two grandchildren.

Natasha Sunday Clarke

Natasha Sunday Clarke was born in Clanton, Alabama, however she is a native of Winston-Salem, North Carolina. Natasha holds a Bachelor of Science degree in Public Relations from North Carolina Agricultural & Technical State University, a Master of Management in Human Resource Management from the University of Phoenix, and a certification in Ministry from the Sonship School of the Firstborn.

In 1997 she enlisted into the United States Army Reserves and later received her commission into the Transportation Corps as a Second Lieutenant. Natasha has been stationed all over the world, to include three combat deployments, two to Iraq and one to Afghanistan. A Lieutenant Colonel, she is currently the Commander of the New England Recruiting Battalion located in Kittery, Maine.

Natasha is involved in numerous organizations to include: Order of the Eastern Star, Zeta Phi Beta Sorority, Incorporated; Association of the United States Army; National Defense Transportation Association; The League of Roses; The ROCKS, Incorporated; and Military Mentors to name a few.

A devoted wife and mother, Natasha is married to Lieutenant Colonel (retired) James Clarke, Jr. and they have two children.

Jeri A. Dyson, M.D.

A native of Washington, DC, Jeri Dyson, M.D. is a physician of Adolescent and Young Adult Medicine, author, and dynamic global speaker. She specializes in sexually transmitted infections and reproductive health. One of today's foremost thinkers of global teen health, Dr. Dyson, is the founding president of the nonprofit, Global Girls Global Women, Inc., where she devotes her full time to national and global leadership programs as an adviser.

Dr. Dyson was the medical expert for BET's Rap-It-Up HIV/AIDS Campaign and has made numerous television appearances on BET, Trinity Broadcasting Network (TBN), Fox 5 Good Day DC, and The CW Network. Dr. Dyson has also been a recurring guest on various radio platforms. In addition, she hosted her own radio talk show, Dr. Jeri Speaks, highlighting "HOT TEEN TOPICS."

Before establishing Global Girls Global Women, Dr. Dyson served as a civilian physician at the Walter Reed National Military Medical Center at Bethesda for 5 years. Her passion for women's health has taken her on medical missions to Ghana, Gambia, and Senegal, West Africa, to name a few. She was also commissioned to Fiji, Papua New Guinea, and Trinidad & Tobago by the U.S. State Department to lecture and develop programs addressing the needs of their youth and women.

Dr. Dyson's first book, An Apple A Day Keeps the Drama Away, was released in 2013. She is currently implementing "The Hummingbird Project," a program designed to introduce girls as global citizens through cultural immersion and international travel.

Anjylla Y. Foster, Ph.D.

Dr. Anjylla Y. Foster is a Midwest native raised in Chicago but a citizen of the world. She is a two-time graduate of the University of Cincinnati where she obtained a Bachelor of Business Administration in two concentrations, Marketing and International Business; and, her Masters of Arts in Communication. Anjylla has a strong love of learning as noted by certificates earned from the University of Pennsylvania in Positive Psychology (2020); Northwestern University in Nonprofit Management (2020), and, from the University of South Florida in Diversity, Equity, and Inclusion (2021). At 30 years of age, Anjylla completed her doctoral degree in Organization Development from Benedictine University. Her research examined "The Transcendent Workplace Experience: An Exploratory Study Enabling Organizations to Cultivate an Engaged, Thriving and Flourishing Workforce." Her continued research focuses on strategies for organizations to enable positive behaviors and experiences in the workplace that lead associates to stronger contributions while exponentially happier.

She has spent most of her nonprofit management career leading operations with diverse teams for cultural institutions and civic spaces, currently with the Museum of Science and Industry in Chicago. She prides herself on being a human resource with expertise that includes job training, coaching, mentoring, professional development, conflict management, and culture curation.

Dr. Foster served Zeta Phi Beta Sorority as the International Vice President responsible for undergraduate programming and currently works on the Associate Board for the Chicago New Moms Organization. In her spare time, she enjoys listening to live music, crafting, reading, and traveling.

Gigi Gilliard

As author of *The Inclusion C.O.D.E.*, *The Loud Brown Round Girl* (2020) and *Hello Beautiful, Get Well Soon* (2021), Gigi is a celebrated public speaker, an accomplished writer, corporate trainer and executive coach. An often-sought-after keynote speaker and Mistress of Ceremonies, Gigi has been an outspoken and prolific DEI&B (diversity, equity, inclusion and belonging) practitioner in the corporate, non-profit, and higher education space for the last decade. She received her Bachelor's degree in Sociology and Communications from Rutgers University, and is pursuing an Executive Masters in Organizational Development from Cornell University's School of Industrial Labor Relations.

A stalwart enemy of exclusion and inequality for any group anywhere, Gigi continues to successfully run her Learning and Development consultancy Gigi Gilliard Development (gigigilliarddevelopment.com)where diversity, equity, inclusion AND belonging is her specialty. She has coined the moniker **DEI&B** and believes that creating the sentiment of belonging is a crucial, and often missed, part of the inclusion conversation.

A native resident New Yorker, she is focused on sharing principles of belongingness and inclusion with those interested in championing these behavioral changes in their workspaces and in their lives. Devoted to her faith, her family and her beloveds, Gigi is often referred to as "our favorite ridiculous Auntie" …and by the sobriquet of 'love monster.'

Dr. Stacie NC Grant

Privately, Dr. Stacie NC Grant often quotes this message from Ghandi "The best way to find yourself, is to lose yourself in the service of others." This is how she has built a global platform of service living her divine calling to LEAD, TEACH and INSPIRE! Dr. Grant has spent countless hours quietly volunteering her time and service in the community through her civic engagement and youth mentorship. She has received numerous awards from the NYS Senate, NYS Assembly, NYC City Council, Office of the Governor of NY, national and local organizations including her most recent recognition as a Woman of Distinction by the Continental Societies, Inc. Her body of work is punctuated by receiving the 2016 Presidential Lifetime Achievement Award for Volunteer Service from our 44th President Barack Obama, an appointment in 2017 as a Fellow of the Most Excellent Order of International Experts (FOIE) and a recipient of the 2019 I CHANGE NATIONS (ICN) World Civility Ambassador Award. In 2021 Dr. Grant was named as one of The Power 50 MWBE Businesses in New York State & New York City, VIP Global Magazine Top 50 Women in Business and The Network Journal's 25 Most Influential Black Women in Business.

Dr. Grant is the Chief Brilliance Officer of C&G Enterprises Unlimited, LLC an MWBE firm that focuses on meeting facilitation and professional development training services. Currently, she is the Facilitator for the JFK Airport Redevelopment Community Advisory Council, a 13 billion dollar redevelopment project: www.CGEUnlimited.com

Additionally, Dr. Grant is the Producer of the annual www.FaithpreneurWeekend.com. She is also a proud Life Member of Zeta Phi Beta Sorority, Inc. and Associate Member of Jack & Jill of America, Inc.

Kristin Harper

Kristin Harper is founder and CEO of Driven to Succeed, LLC, which helps drive business growth through market research, brand strategy consulting, and brainstorming facilitation for Fortune 500 companies and leading brands.

An award-winning businesswoman, Kristin went from college intern to Global VP of a Fortune 15 company in her 30s. A classically trained marketer who built her career at Procter & Gamble, The Hershey Company and Cardinal Health, she's led global iconic brands including Crest®, Oral-B®, and Hershey's KISSES®.

Kristin and her team have worked with diverse clients across many industries, including Clorox, Colgate-Palmolive, General Mills, HEB, Kellogg's, Kraft, Levi's, Merck, Nestle, Nike, Novartis, Procter & Gamble, PepsiCo, Pfizer, Saatchi & Saatchi, Safeway, Toyota, and many more.

Author of *The Heart of a Leader: 52 Emotional Intelligence Insights to Advance Your Career,* Kristin provides keynotes and leadership training to rising leaders at companies, conferences, and through online training and coaching.

She serves on the Board of Trustees at Florida A&M University and is actively involved in her church and the community as an active lifetime member of Delta Sigma Theta Sorority, Inc., minister at her church, and Co-Founder/Board President of Pacesetters Unlimited, Inc., which provides mentoring and HBCU scholarships to African American youth. Kristin received her bachelor's and MBA degrees from Florida A&M University. She and her husband are the proud parents of three children.

For more information, visit www.DriventoSucceedLLC.com or www.KristinHarper.com.

Sharon P. Jarrett

Armed with an Accounting degree from Tuskegee University and 16 years in Corporate America at IBM, managing large scale global projects in excess of $35M annually, since 2005 Sharon Jarrett has served as President & CEO of Jarrett Affairs, an award-winning event management & production firm. As a results-oriented event strategist, Sharon continues to design world-class events (Live, Virtual & Hybrid) globally while managing high performance event teams remotely to consistently deliver multiple events simultaneously ON TIME, ON TARGET and ON BUDGET!

Known as a Game Changer and often referred to as the "Olivia Pope" of events, Sharon's heartbeat is the "flawless execution" of a well-designed event plan. Her detailed approach to producing events has allowed her to attract clients from across the US including Fortune 500 companies, established small business owners, mission driven non-profit organizations as well as accomplished individuals, including the NBA, Steve Harvey Worldwide, Judge Glenda Hatchett, The Coca Cola Company, Jack & Jill of America, Inc. and the National Black MBA Association to name a few. However, as a small business owner, Sharon prides herself on providing the same level of expertise & commitment to other small business owners as well. She consistently meets her clients' business objectives while creating brand experiences where both the hosts and attendees lose count of the times, they say WOW! Sharon and her husband Steve reside in Charlotte, NC and are the proud parents of two young adults Royce & Tori.

For more information on Jarrett Affairs, please visit www. JarrettAffairs.com

Chonya Johnson

CHONYA JOHNSON is America's 5 Minute Advocate, Author and Government Affairs consultant. She has trained thousands of citizens advocates from all over the United States to effectively influence Congress, state, and local governments. She is a former hill policy staffer, who worked for nearly two decades in the United States Congress. While serving in Congress she gained valuable, first-hand experiences of the intricacies of government practices and the concerns of advocates, constituents and businesses. Chonya develops interactive advocacy training seminars for citizens and organizations to prepare them to effectively advocate for their issues.

Chonya is a fighter and champion for everyday people and organizations that face tough issues. Her real-life experiences and insight on what works, while being of service, allowed her to survive the game of politics beyond political parties and bureaucracy. She fought diligently to get constituents a second chance to plead their case before federal, state and local agencies.

She designed the 5 Minute Advocate program and facilitates key-contact networks, lobby days, and training programs for national associations and organizations, including the National Organization Black Elected Leaders, American Association of University Women, Jack and Jill of America, Inc., Zeta Phi Beta Sorority Inc., The MAC Campaign and a host of women, community groups and democratic clubs.

Mrs. Johnson is the author of several books on advocacy, leadership and campaign success. Chonya holds a Masters Degree in Political Science from University of Northern Iowa and is a recent recipient of the Education Pioneer Graduate Fellowship, SpeakerCon-Advocate of the Year & The League of Women Voters Chatman Rising Star award.

Marilyn Johnson

Marilyn Johnson is founder of *MarilynJspeaks.com*, serving as a principal spokesperson, keynote speaker, facilitator or emcee, and as a global ambassador to promote and support women in leadership. Prior to this she served as the CEO of the International Women's Forum, with a mission to support women in prominent senior leadership roles internationally. She retired from IBM as the Vice President, Market Development, based in New York, NY. In this capacity, she led an organization responsible for developing IBM's strategy for marketing to businesses owned or operated by Asians, Blacks, Hispanics, Native Americans and Women in the Americas. In that role she expanded her mission to include women-owned and women-led businesses in selected markets around the globe. She held executive positions in key IBM business units and has had management and operational responsibility in North America, the Middle East, Africa, Latin America and Asia.

She also served on the Executive Board of the United States Council for Better Business Bureaus and the Executive Boards of the Asian Pacific Islander American Scholarship Foundation, the National Council of Negro Women and American Airlines Marketing Advisory Council. Ms. Johnson has been a featured speaker for numerous professional organizations around the world, including The IWF Executive Development Roundtable in Toronto, Canada; the World Diversity Conference, City of Prague in the Czech Republic; the Black Women Executive Roundtable hosted by the Mayor of Paris, France; B.I.G. (Blacks in Government), Washington, DC; AWAKE in Mysore, India; and the Cornerstone Conference in Johannesburg, South Africa and she spoke at the DLD Media Conference in Munich, Germany; the Women Leader's Forum in Douala, Cameroon and the Women Chiefs Forum in Canberra, Australia.

Melissa I. Walton Jones

Melissa I. Walton Jones is the Director of Finance for a tri-state Metropolitan Planning Organization managing awarded funds of more than $50M. Serving for-profit and non-profit corporations as a career professional over the last 20+ years, she is currently responsible for accounting, financial planning and analysis, annual budgeting, financial reporting, and overall business administration and serves as a member of senior leadership providing counsel to the CEO. She obtained an MBA from the University of Missouri, with an International Finance Residency in China.

A native of Holly Springs, MS, Melissa matriculated and graduated from Rust College, a historically Black college (HBCU) in her hometown. Holly Springs is known for its southern hospitality and rich history dating back to the Civil War. It is also the birthplace of Ida B. Wells-Barnett and home to The Ida B. Wells-Barnett Museum. Sharing the same birthday as Ms. Wells-Barnett, Melissa grew up with special attention to her rich history and activism. She has always believed that good things have and continue to come from Mississippi.

A woman of many talents, Melissa is a licensed minister and could sing before she could talk. She grew up listening to Gospel and R&B/ Soul singers, from Shirley Caesar to Whitney Houston. An anointed songstress, gifted composer, and a deeply affectionate lover of music, Melissa is a collaborative servant-leader. She enjoys global travel, singing, reading, golfing, writing, and spending quality time with her husband and life partner, Lester Jones, son Darion, daughter Dawsonne, and fur baby Lola.

Helen Hope Kimbrough

 Helen Hope Kimbrough is a consultant, reading evangelist, literacy advocate, & racial equity champion. She journeyed into writing and publishing children's books because she was unable to find books with diverse characters especially for boys of color. In 2005, she founded her independent publishing company, AK Classics LLC, to create relatable and cultural content for children and families of color.

As an author of four multicultural children's books and a publisher of numerous book titles in various genres, Helen has committed herself to literacy initiatives and delves into the importance of representation, inclusion, and unique experiences relative to storytelling.

One of Helen's favorite quotes is by Dr. Martin Luther King, Jr. which states, "Everybody can be great -- because anybody can serve." She is purpose-driven and devoted to making an impact.

Helen currently resides in Charlotte, North Carolina with her husband and is a proud mother of two sons.

Marjorie A. Kinard

Marjorie A. Kinard is a much sought after speaker, community activist and fund raiser. She has been an educator in the public schools of the District of Columbia, and an administrator at Livingstone College as Director of Alumni Affairs, Director of Enrollment Management, and Dean of Student Affairs. At Barber-Scotia College she served as Director of Public Relations. Most recently she has been involved in the field of Early Childhood Education as Director of the Shiloh Baptist Church Child Development Center, Washington, D. C. She was employed at the East of the River Health Association, Community Health care, Inc. as Director of Special Projects, Director of Adolescent Health Care, Executive Assistant to the Director and Director of Marketing. She moderated the weekly radio show "Health Talk" on WYCB.

She is a member of John Wesley AME Zion Church, and had served as a member of the Board of Trustees, a Class Leader and member of the Parent Body WHOMS. She also serves, presently, as a member of the Deaconess Board, Stewardess Board and is the church Events Planner. She is a member of the National Council of Negro Women, a Life Member of both the Livingstone College National Alumni Association, and the Barber Scotia College National Alumni Association. She is also a member of the National Association for the Education of Young Children and the Washington Association of Child Care Centers. She is a Life Member of Delta Sigma Theta Sorority, Inc. and has served on its National Executive Board.

Marjorie Kinard is the widow of Rev. John R. Kinard, and the mother of three daughters, Sarah, Joy and Hope, and a grandmother of five.

Marie Turner McCleave

Marie Turner McCleave is the "Godmother" of the Livingstone College Class of '76. Elected as the Homecoming Queen during her senior year of college, she has never strayed far from her gift of helping people especially her family. Her history of building and maintaining relationships is at the center of her existence as demonstrated by the 43 years of marriage to her college sweetheart, Ron.

She is a community servant and advocate for people which defines her career in positions in the fields of health education, counseling and social with work history at Planned Parenthood, Grady Memorial Hospital and the Council on Battered Women. Her degrees from Livingstone College and an M.S.W. from the University of Connecticut School of Social Work prepared her to provide care to people who needed her expertise, her passion. A member of Delta Sigma Theta, she served as president of her chapter with the objective to provide greater service to the community.

Marie's daughter and her husband have blessed the McCleave legacy with 3 children who are her pride and joy. They currently reside in Atlanta, GA.

Tamara McGill McFarland

Tamara is an advocate for women's right to choose motherhood on their own time. Having had her daughter in her late 30's and her son in her 40's, she often speaks to women about what she considers "reproductive insurance" by planning for motherhood.

Like many women choosing to have children later in life, she earlier focused on her career in fashion and entertainment as a model and entertainment show co-host.

As both a mother and entrepreneur, she is the Co-Founder of Preserve Perfect, a self-care product line providing natural skincare and undergarment support for expectant mothers.

Tamara enjoys exploring different cuisines and considers herself a "part-time" vegan. Additionally, she enjoys bantering with her husband, spending time with her 'Motown Loving Babies' and yoga to keep her grounded.

Make sure to stay tuned as this mommy on the move will be launching 'Tamara's Taste'; a lifestyle blog sharing her palette for all things food, fashion, and travel.

You can find and follow Tamara spreading her love and light on Instagram @tamaramcgillmcfarland.

Alana Ward Robinson

Alana Ward Robinson is the President and CEO of Robinson Group Consulting (RGC) which she founded in 2004. RGC is a management consulting firm which specializes in developing roadmaps to help organizations think strategically about technology investments, build operational capacity for growth, and lead change.

Alana is an enterprise-oriented CIO and strategic Technology expert who finds solutions to innovate organizations and solve complex business problems by leveraging expertise gained from a career working with and in a wide range of industries with companies from start-up to Fortune 500 companies including multiple executive roles at IBM, Coors, Sara Lee and R. R. Donnelley. She enjoys bridging the gap between executives to understand and become comfortable with new technologies, advising on the right technology investments while taking both the risks and opportunities into account to deliver increased productivity and the ability to scale. She and her team have led multiple large-scale global transformation initiatives.

Alana serves in a variety of civic and not-for-profit organizations, including World Food Program HQ (Rome, Italy) – IT Advisory Board; Brighter Horizon Foundation, Board Chair; Chicago's Metropolitan Planning Council; Girls Inc. of Chicago, Board Secretary; The National Hospice Foundation; The Executive Leadership Council and Foundation Boards; and The African American Experience Fund. She is a Founder and member of the Information Technology Senior Management Forum (ITSMF).

Alana received a B.A. in Applied Mathematics and Computer Science from Grambling State University, Grambling, LA. She and her husband, E. O'Neal Robinson, have two adult sons and reside in Chicago, IL and Irving, TX.

Jylla Moore Tearte, Ph.D.

Dr. Jylla Moore Tearte is an award-winning author who has published, authored and/or coached twenty-seven books and publications. She views **PIVOT** as an assignment that continues her legacy of world-class service espoused during her tenure as the International President of Zeta Phi Beta Sorority, Inc. A former corporate sales and marketing executive at IBM, her philanthropic work as co-founder of the Tearte Family Foundation has kept her in the forefront of issues related to education, social advocacy and initiatives that impact women. Chairing Zeta's Centennial Celebration during 2020, while challenging, was a dream fulfilled on January 16, 2020 when Zeta celebrated its Centennial Founders' Day on both the campus of Howard University and that evening at the National Museum for African American History and Culture where she and her husband Curtis are major donors.

Recognized as a 2018 inductee into The HistoryMakers, she is a lifetime member of the NAACP, NCNW, Urban League, NBM-BAA, Livingstone College Alumni Association and Zeta Phi Beta Sorority, Inc. In 2016, the Consortium for Graduate Study in Business honored her work with the Wallace Jones Lifetime Achievement Award. Jylla and Curtis cherish their time with two amazing daughters and twin infant grandsons. *When I THINK of HOME*, her story, shares from the pandemic rear-view mirror that nothing was more important than her personal journey HOME, closer to her family and friends.

Monique N. Tookes

Known for her no-nonsense approach, radical honesty, and ability to relate to any audience, Monique Nicole Tookes demonstrates wisdom beyond her years. A native of Detroit, MI, today she resides in Jacksonville, FL, with her husband, Cyrus III, of over 23 years. Together, they are the loving parents of nine beautiful children.

She is a Parent/Family Educational Advocate who has served the Duval County Public School System for over 15 years. Those bevy of experiences led her to run for the District 6 seat on the Duval County School Board. Monique is the founder of the Titus Women's Fellowship, a ministry that activates ladies to become the wives, mothers, and leaders God called them to be.

As Director of the Family Empowerment Ministry at the Potter's House International Ministries, Monique is a visionary and sought-after speaker with a proven track record of empowering people to serve for the betterment of the home, community and educational system.

Audrey Washington

Ms. Washington is a sophomore in college. Having matriculated at an all-girl's high school, she found her voice for issues that she is passionate about. Working at a law firm throughout her high school years, she became very interested in forensics and plans to complete a degree in criminal justice. It is her life's mission to honor her family's name as a daughter of immigrants. Ms. Washington's passion for helping others inspired her to offer the story of her freshman year in college during the pandemic of 2020.

Acknowledgments

This visionary book project is the result of several individuals adopting the vision for their own. The energy shared by the team of collaborators was validation of the importance of sharing the stories of women who had navigated pivotal moments during the pandemic. We offer THANKS to those who have joined us on this incredible journey.

Jarrett Affairs and Crystal Stairs, Inc. acknowledge:

Contributing Authors: THANK YOU for answering the call! More so, THANK YOU for reaching deep within to share the dark moments that will allow others to gain the hope and confidence that they too can find the light. It's through your eyes and your experience that others will find their story and the energy to push forward.

Marjorie A. Kinard, Chonya Johnson, Alana Ward Robinson, Dr. Stacie NC Grant, Helen Hope Kimbrough, Gigi Gilliard, Marilyn Johnson, Rev. Teraleen Campbell, Marie Turner McCleave, Tamara McGill McFarland, Natasha Sunday Clarke, Audrey Washington, Monique N. Tookes, Melissa I. Walton Jones, Kristin Harper, Dr. Jeri Dyson, Anjylla Y. Foster, Ph.D., Vesta Godwin Clark

Book Production Team: When we called, our trusted resources responded and immediately supported this effort with their expertise. We expressly thank:

- Reginald Knox, Presyce Media, for providing the technology processes and expertise;
- E. Claudette Freeman, Pecan Tree Publishing, for expert editing to pull out the stories;

- Daniel Barrozo, the Ink Studio, for book covers, and interior page layout and design;
- Dreama Kemp, Cover Artist, for depicting the masks that women wear.

Sharon acknowledges:

Corrie Watts Blackmon and Eloise McGlothin Jones, my dearly departed grandmothers who now sit amongst our ancestors. You both left us too soon but loved our family hard, worked hard and endured far too much during the stench of the Jim Crow South for your children, grandchildren, and great-grandchildren to be anything but successful. The memories I have of each of you guided me through this process. I knew once I started, there was no way I would give up completing it. Continue to rest in power and know that your little bossy granddaughter is doing OKAY!

When I prayed for a **daughter**, I could have never imagined the blessing my Tori would be. In part, I am sharing these stories for you Babygirl. Your star is so bright; I pray that through these stories you navigate your own journey with a heightened awareness on the importance of self-care.

To my chapter and line-sisters (Spring '87) of the Gamma Kappa chapter of Alpha Kappa Alpha Sorority, Inc, on the campus of Tuskegee University; simply being connected to such amazing women has been one of my greatest treasures. *"Meet me around the tree."*

To every woman who picks up this book and reads it, THANK YOU for making it all worthwhile. May your days be filled with Self-Care and Sisterhood.

Dr. Jylla acknowledges:

Curtis, Anjylla and Maxine, you provided the space, coaching and timeless hours of listening to dive into these stories with a life of experiences that allow this process to flow to completion! You are loved more than words could ever explain. THANK YOU for guiding me HOME and for the ever present imagery of Billy Porter and M J Rodriguez singing HOME as they helped people find HOME in the brilliant story of Pose.

To my NETWORKs that WERK!

Sisters of Zeta Phi Beta Sorority, Inc. who inspire me daily with our more than 100 years of uninterrupted service to our communities; to my Divine 9 family who see beyond colors to the heart of serving together; Michelle Adkins for introducing me to the virtual spiritual family of Alfred Street Baptist Church in Alexandria, VA where together we had previously physically grieved the loss of Margaret Turner whose name I call in remembrance of the inspirational moments we shared together as we observed her commitment to the National Museum of African American History and Culture; Pastor Howard-John Wesley whose innovative virtual ministry, ministered to my mind, body and soul with the never-ending series of provocative teaching and preaching; Pastor Damon Lynch of New Prospect Baptist Church in Cincinnati, Ohio who connected my spiritual walk during the pandemic with virtual access to learning and teaching; to Marie Turner McCleave who provided constant networking with the Livingstone College – Class of '76; and, to my friends and family who called just to check in on the regular or posted life's special moments as we navigated the pandemic.

To David Roberts, Whitney's Bodyguard, who encouraged me to have courage after a very long conversation when I asked, "What can I do to prevent a repeat of this story?" He replied: "Just do the work you have been called to do that you just shared with me." This book has shown me my work. I'll always love you David for that moment in time in paradise. Dr. Kristian Aloma and Dr. Mark Rittenberg, professors in the Northwestern University Non-Profit Executive Certification program, THANK YOU for teaching me the power of story… and the release of emotions to tell stories. Forever grateful for the villain and the victim debate… curtains up, curtains down!

Mental Health Resource Guide

Find a Mental Health Provider:
- Psychology Today
  https://www.psychologytoday.com/us
- Therapy For Black Girls
  https://therapyforblackgirls.com/
- Better Help
  https://www.betterhelp.com/
- Talkspace
  https://www.talkspace.com/

Maternal Mental Health
Postpartum Support International
https://www.postpartum.net

National Alliance on Mental Illness Hotline (NAMI)
800-950-6264

Suicide/Crisis
National Suicide Prevention Hotline
(800) 273-8255

Substance Abuse and Mental Health Helpline
1-800-HELP (4357)

Other Resources or things to consider:
Most Employers offer an Employee Assistance Program (EAP). This program can provide free Mental Health/Behavioral Health Sessions for you and your family.

Call your Insurance Company and ask these questions:
1. Does my health insurance include mental health service benefits?
2. Do I have a co-pay? If so, how much is my co-pay?
3. Is there a limit on how many sessions I can have? If so, what is the limit?
4. Is my desired provider an in-network provider?

Compiled by:
Tahlisha S. Dorsey, MSW LISW-S
T.dorsey@serenitytherapyservices.com
Serenitytherapyservices.com

What's Your Story?

The authors of *PIVOT.* were inspired to focus on their passion by remembering and writing down just a snippet of their story. Please take the time to jot down your thoughts in this section. We encourage you to move closer to your next chapter. Take notes from the stories of the authors who resonated with you and determine your action plan. Find an accountability partner; begin a sister circle; discuss in your book club; establish a network of like-minded individuals who share your journey; and/or, hire a coach or a professional provider to help chart your path forward.

Capture your moments and PIVOT.

The Big Five Pivotal Questions...

1. Write down a story that caused you to PIVOT.

_____

_____

_____

_____

_____

_____

_____

_____

_____

_____

2. What were you most proud of when you "changed" your
    previous way of approaching the situation?

    _____

    _____

    _____

    _____

    _____

    _____

    _____

    _____

3. What did you "let go" that you have not missed and
    won't bring back?

    _____

    _____

    _____

    _____

    _____

    _____

    _____

    _____

4. What do you aspire to do more of in life?

_____

_____

_____

_____

_____

_____

_____

_____

5. What music is on your playlist of life that inspires you to dream and achieve?

_____

_____

_____

_____

_____

_____

_____

_____

10 Goals to Reach in the Next 90 Days

What are the goals you most want to set for yourself for the next 90 days? Please select only those goals, which you really want, not the ones you should, could, ought, or might want. Look deep inside and then write down your 10 personal and professional goals. Write down 3 actions or strategies for each goal and discuss these with your accountability partner. When you set the right goals for yourself, you should feel excited, a little nervous, ready and willing to go for it!! Don't select the goals you historically have chosen, but never reached, unless you're in a much better position to reach them now.

Start Date	Finish Date	The Specific Measurable Goal		Actions/Strategies	Status
__/__/__	__/__/__	1.		1. 2. 3.	☐
__/__/__	__/__/__	2.		1. 2. 3.	☐
__/__/__	__/__/__	3.		1. 2. 3.	☐
__/__/__	__/__/__	4.		1. 2. 3.	☐
__/__/__	__/__/__	5.		1. 2. 3.	☐
__/__/__	__/__/__	6.		1. 2. 3.	☐

_/_/_	_/_/_	7.		1. 2. 3.	☐
_/_/_	_/_/_	8.		1. 2. 3.	☐
_/_/_	_/_/_	9.		1. 2. 3.	☐
_/_/_	_/_/_	10.		1. 2. 3.	☐

What are the personal/professional benefits to you of accomplishing these goals?

1.	_____
2.	_____
3.	_____

© Crystal Stairs, Inc.

Stay Connected

Web: https://CrystalStairsPublishers.com/PIVOT

Email: Publishers@Crystal-Stairs.com

Twitter: #PIVOTPeriod
#PIVOTtoPassionBook

Instagram: _CrystalStairs

Facebook: Facebook.com/crystalstairsinc

Author Businesses and Partners

Please reach out to our authors and partners if you would like to discuss their services. We do not endorse or receive compensation for this recognition but trust that this lead engine will be productive for our network and our audience.

Author Businesses		
Rev. Teraleen Campbell	TeraleenCampbell.com	Author, Coach, Intercessor, Speaker
Vesta Godwin Clark	StJamesSSC.org	Executive Director
Dr. Jeri Dyson	GlobalGirlsGlobalWomen.org	Physician, Author, Global Speaker
Gigi Gilliard	GigiGilliardDevelopment.com	DEI&B Facilitator, Executive Coach, Speaker, Author
Dr. Stacie NC Grant	DestinyDesignersUniversity.com	Faithpreneurs Business Coach, Speaker, Author
Kristin Harper	DriventoSucceedLLC.com	Leadership Development, Author
Sharon P. Jarrett	JarrettAffairs.com	Event Design and Productions
Chonya Johnson	ChonyaJohnson.com	Advocate, Government Affairs Consultant, Author
Marilyn Johnson	MarilynJSpeaks.com	Speaker, Consultant

Author Businesses

Melissa I. Walton Jones	MelissaWaltonJones.com	Speaker, Business Consultant
Helen Hope Kimbrough	akclassicstories.com	Publisher, Author
Tamara McGill McFarland	preserveperfect.com	Mom-to-be Skin Care
Alana Ward Robinson	One-RGC.com	Technology Consulting
Jylla Moore Tearte, Ph.D.	Crystal-Stairs.com	Executive/Encore Leadership Coach, Author, Speaker
Monique N. Tookes	MoniqueTookes.com	Family Education Advocate, Author

Partners

Daniel Barrozo	danielb@theInkStudio.net	Book Production
Gionni "Stylo" Carr	Instagram: gionnistylomusic	Original Music
E. Claudette Freeman	PecanTreeBooks.com	Editor
Dreama Kemp	DreamaFineArt.com	Commissioned Art
Reginald Knox	PresyceMedia.com	Technology, Design
Ashley Little	AshleyLittleEnterprises.com	Marketing
Addison Wright	AddisonJWright.com	Filmmaker

Made in United States
North Haven, CT
24 February 2022

16445224R00085